# SAVAGE SHEPHERDS

'I am increasingly concerned at how often I meet de-churched Christians, those that have dropped out of church, many bruised and bleeding. Sadly, Church leaders can be well-meaning, but misguided. Spiritual abuse is toxic and shackles its victims oppressively.

My friend Adam Harbinson's story is compelling reading and shocking – along the way there are many thorns, but the fragrant healing aroma of Christ's liberating love permeates through.

I urge every church leader to read this book.'

J.John, evangelist and author

'Adam tells a story of spiritual abuse which is tragic and all too common. We all know people who should read it. His book will serve as a warning to many and provides support to those for whom the warning came too late.'

Ken Blue, author of *Healing Spiritual Abuse*

'Though I find solace in places I never could have imagined . . . the quiet sprinkling of my child's head in baptism . . . a gospel choir drunk on the Holy Spirit in Memphis, or the back of a cathedral in Rome watching the first cinematographers play with light and colour in stained-glass stories of the Passion . . . I am still amazed at how big, how enormous a love and a mystery God is – and how small are the minds that attempt to corral this life force into rules and taboos, cults and sects . . . mercifully, God transcends the church which is, I think, the subject of the book.'

Bono, U2

'"There was a little girl who had a little curl right in the mid-dle of her forehead and when she was good she was very, very good and when she was bad she was horrid." Surely this is true of the church as well.

C.S. Lewis would often complain about why God didn't make people of the kind of stuff that wouldn't go so bad. However, he soon realised that the better stuff something is made of, the greater its potential in both directions. Indeed the best of people can also be the worst of people.

The local church, because it is made of great stuff, has the potential of doing irreparable harm in people's lives. In his new book, Adam Harbinson shares his journey that shows both the power of spiritual abuse operating within the church as well as the grace, forgiveness and healing that can and should play through local churches as they reflect God as he truly is.

I heartily recommend it.'

Phil Baker, Senior Minister, Riverview Church, Perth

'There is justifiable anger in Adam's writings, and he has a pretty good handle on the role that the church should be play-ing.'

Tony Campolo, author and speaker

# SAVAGE SHEPHERDS

One Man's Story of Overcoming Spiritual
Abuse

**Adam Harbinson**

**Authentic**

**LONDON – ATLANTA – HYDERABAD**

12 11 10 09 08 07 06    7 6 5 4 3 2 1

First published 2006 by Authentic Media
9 Holdom Avenue, Bletchley, Milton Keynes, MK1 1QR, UK
Lynnwood Drive, Tyrone, GA
OM Authentic Media
Medchal Road, Jeedimetla Village, Secunderabad 500 055, A. P.
www.authenticmedia.co.uk
Authentic Media is a division of Send the Light Ltd., a company
limited by guarantee (registered charity no. 270162)

**British Library Cataloguing in Publication Data**
A catalogue record for this book is available from the
British Library

ISBN-13 978-1-86024-574-9
ISBN-10 1-86204-574-9

Cover Design by fourninezero design.
Print Management by Adare Carwin
Printed in Great Britain by J.H. Haynes & Co., Sparkford

# Contents

# ACKNOWLEDGEMENTS

This book, like any other, has one name on it as the author, but like any other, it is the product of the combined efforts of many. I will name only three. I am grateful, firstly, to my wife Pauline, for her endless patience as together we read and re-read early manuscripts, piecing together thoughts and experiences, trying to place them in order of some coherence.

Secondly, to my editor and now friend Alison Hull, my heartfelt thanks. Her wisdom and ability to spot how a single word can change the meaning of a sentence have been of inestimable value.

And thirdly, my great friend J.John, without whose intervention it's hard to see how the book would have seen the light of day. Thank you.

Adam Harbinson

# INTRODUCTION

Imagine a Christian community in which each male member is expected to submit to the authority of a specific pastor, usually referred to as his 'shepherd'. Wives are required to submit to their husbands, regardless of how they are treated by them, and single females don't count for much. Submission is demonstrated by serving the shepherd: doing his gardening, babysitting, helping with household chores, etc., and it's not an option, if membership is to be taken seriously. Submission to the shepherd's authority is also signified by publicly tithing directly to him. At the end of each month, the accredited shepherds line up across the front of the church building, while the male members file dutifully forward and, one by one, hand their shepherd a cheque or a wad of notes.

The symbolism is important here. The sheep pays his tithes via his shepherd because his shepherd is seen as God's lieutenant in a chain of command that stretches all the way back to heaven itself. The shepherd is seen as God's delegated spokesman, and any attempt by the sheep to hear from God without the intervention or approval of the shepherd is frowned upon. That is spiritual abuse.

Imagine a young married couple who have recently become Christians. Jim loves the church, Shirley isn't quite so sure. Night after night she sits alone at home watching the television, waiting for her husband to come home from yet another meeting – and the marriage begins to unravel. At her instigation, they visit the pastor in the hope of finding a compromise. 'You have a clear choice, Jim,' says the man of God, after a frank and open discussion. 'The service of the Lord, or your wife.' Of course the pastor knows best and the marriage is over. That is gross spiritual abuse.

Imagine a young lady, in her late twenties, who has dedicated her life to the church she was born into, a church that her parents helped establish. She teaches Sunday school and is a youth worker. Her marriage of three years ends in tears, through no fault of hers; she tried hard to hold it together. And as she struggles with the emotional turmoil of it all – the rejection, the disappointment, the implied guilt – she is visited by her pastor. Comforting her is not on his agenda. As a divorcee, she's welcome to remain as a member of God's family, but there's no opportunity for her to serve in his church. That's abuse.

Imagine a Christian community whose self-appointed leader has such a clear sense of calling and becomes so blinkered in his single-mindedness that he borders on fanaticism. He will achieve what he believes God wants him to achieve, regardless of those who get hurt in the process. Anyone who questions his beliefs or methods is accused of opposing the purposes of God. Negative comments about his style of leadership are seen as attempts to undermine his authority. He reacts badly to criticism, constructive or otherwise, interpreting it as a personal attack. Those who are not for him are against him, and against God as well, since he is the Lord's anointed. That's an abusive church.

Abuse happens when someone has power over another and uses that power to hurt. Spiritual abuse occurs when an individual's spiritual life is systematically damaged by religious leaders who use their authority to control, coerce or manipulate God's people for their own purposes, while making it look as though they are God's purposes. Spiritual abusers place themselves in a chain of command above God's people. But spiritual abuse is nothing new. The prophet Ezekiel railed against it in his day, and Jesus berated the Pharisees for their abusive practices that were designed to create a gulf between God and the common man. Today's church is no different. It too is littered with countless broken and bruised lives. I was there, and this is my story: one of fear and confusion, anger and betrayal.

\* \* \* \*

I have a special concern for you church leaders. I know what it's like to be a leader, in on Christ's sufferings as well as the coming glory. Here's my concern: that you care for God's flock with all the diligence of a shepherd. Not because you have to, but because you want to please God. Not calculating what you can get out of it, but acting spontaneously. Not bossily telling others what to do, but tenderly showing them the way. (1 Pet. 5:1–3, *The Message*).

# CHAPTER 1

# THE BEGINNING OF THE END

I had a reputation of being a hard-nosed, hard-drinking, fast-living, moderately successful businessman. My wife dragged me, heel marks all the way, to what I regarded as an odd little religious group that I tolerated for a couple of hours on an occasional Saturday evening; a sad waste of good partying time. 'The River of Life Fellowship' as we shall call it, whose senior pastor was Tom, was a charismatic church, associated with the shepherding movement as it flourished in the 1970s and 1980s.

Tom's wife, Brenda, and my wife, Daphne, were best friends. They had grown up together, and although I had a certain respect for Brenda, I had little time for her husband or his Fellowship. To me, he was a self-appointed despot, devoid of emotion and compassion, a man whose life was devoted to playing power games.

However, it had been brought to Tom's attention that I was being unfaithful to my wife and he didn't approve. In my view it was none of his business, but he thought it was, so he visited me in my office one Wednesday morning in 1980, presumably to straighten me out. He was nervous but resolute and when my body language indicated that he was unwelcome and was soon to be evicted from my personal space, he reminded me that Brenda and Daphne were good friends who met regularly for coffee. Brenda felt she was being insincere and two-faced when Daphne talked to her about her 'good husband'. She knew I wasn't . . . 'And,' said Tom, 'we're fast coming to the point where Brenda will have to tell her the truth.' That sounded to me like a threat and I didn't respond too kindly to threats.

My body language exploded and Tom was back on the street with my index finger still wagging inches from his nose, amid many decibels. However, before he trundled off, disconsolate, he turned to me and said, 'The trouble with you, Adam, is that you don't realise the seriousness of your situation' – and then he added 'and your children will replicate your behaviour'. That cut deep but nonetheless the stout front door of my office only just managed to hang onto its hinges.

How could I live with myself if my two little boys, one seven years old, the other just eight weeks, were to turn out like me? And what if my three-year-old daughter were to grow up and embrace my seedy values?

There was no way Tom could have known that the previous Monday morning, my life had reached such a low point that I had to stretch up to touch bottom. The prayers of a faithful old mother and a despairing wife were bearing fruit and, for the first time in many years, I called out to God. As my wife was doing the school-run that morning, I fell to my knees beside my bed. 'O God,' I prayed, 'I hate the life I'm living. If you can do anything with this wild, unscrupulous man, please do, for I can't.' But within minutes, as I heard her car sweep back into the drive, I repositioned myself where I was happiest, in the fast lane of the rat race.

However, the next couple of days saw a succession of people, some of whom I hadn't seen for years, led by the same invisible cord, either call me on the phone or visit me in my office. Their message was the same, 'Adam, it's time you got yourself sorted out!'

So by Wednesday the stage had been set for Tom's missionary expedition. My wife was surprised when I told her that he had called on me, and of course I was selective in what I related to her of our conversation, but I made it clear that I was furious. I worked in the financial services business and of the twenty or so men with whom I shared an office, four were in the 'Mafia', our derogatory name for the River of Life Fellowship. Stories abounded of men who believed they had to consult their pastor before deciding to buy a new washing machine, have a holiday or change the car. 'Well,' I scoffed, 'if that's the way they want to run their pathetic lives, that's their business, but if Tom thinks he can poke his nose into my private affairs like that, he is very wrong. I'm not one of his sheep!'

However, next morning as I sat behind my desk, the Holy Spirit hit me on the back of my head with his celestial cudgel and for the second time in a week I fell to my knees. This time I was weeping like a baby and crying out to God for mercy – a wonderful, if unconventional, introduction to the God who is eternally and extravagantly 'merciful and gracious, he is slow to get angry and full of unfailing love' (Ps. 103:8). I left my office that morning with tears streaming down my face. And in fairness to Tom, he reflected a degree of God's compassion and mercy, for in less than an hour he and I were praying together in the front room of his home: the man whom I had forcibly ejected from my office not twenty-four hours earlier.

Conversions can be life-changing. Mine was dramatic: the excessive drinking and partying stopped immediately. The affair I had tried to end a number of times died instantly and, wonder of wonders, my family and I joined Tom's 'odd little religious group'.

Daphne and I had been married for about ten years. My profligate lifestyle had taken its toll on our relationship, but here was an opportunity for a fresh start. I needed to decide how much I should tell her of what had been going on. It was the most obvious thing in the world to me to be totally honest. I knew it would be tough on her and I recognised the risk that she might leave me, but the alternative would be for me to live a lie. I would then be condemning myself to a life of fear and insecurity. What if someone else were to tell her? What if the young lady whom I had used for my gratification and then unceremoniously dumped were to fulfil the saying 'Hell hath no fury like a woman scorned'? That apart, Daphne was entitled to know the truth about the wretch she had been married to. She had the right to decide whether or not she wanted the marriage to continue. Since I had not yet been taught that I was obliged to consult my shepherd about such grave matters as this, I prayed about what I should do. And as I did, in my mind's eye I saw a lighthouse, crumbling and in need of rebuilding from the foundation up. I'm no builder, but I guess that if all the rubble and coral and decaying seaweed were not scraped away before rebuilding commenced, the new structure would never be stable. No, it must be stripped right down to the bare rock. It was a very vivid picture. And in the same way, I realised that the only way in which our marriage could be rebuilt, risky as it might be, was for me to be totally honest about my past. I needed to tell her, 'This is the type of man I've really been. I'm sorry. I promise things will be different; I promise it will never happen again. If you can forgive me, then we'll start afresh. If you cannot, I understand.'

Tom's view, however, was different. He was adamant. 'Don't say anything. There's no need for her ever to know.' That, to me, sounded both deceitful and short-sighted. It also sounded out of character, for only days before he was threatening that Brenda would tell her everything. But I followed my heart. I was truthful and our marriage survived. I felt secure because there were no skeletons in my cupboard. My wife was secure because she trusted that she had heard the worst and because if someone ever told her of my shenanigans, she could have said, 'Yes, I know. Adam told me.'

But I had been a member of the Fellowship for less than a week and already I was feeling disappointed and a little confused. I had found it necessary to go against the advice of the senior leader of my new church and I didn't want it to be like that. Was there a question mark over Tom's integrity or was I missing something?

Slowly, over the weeks and months that followed, I began to see things that didn't quite stack up and they bothered me. But I chose to ignore them because life had become immeasurably better for my family and me. I had three children at that stage: Simon, Sarah and Timothy, and almost immediately we were assimilated into our new family. The strong sense of community was very positive, to the extent that gradually, almost all of our non-fellowship relationships were eclipsed. We saw no danger in being progressively separated from those on the outside, former friends and family who might have asked awkward questions or given alternative points of view.

In fact, we valued the all-embracing social side of it all. There was always something going on: barbecues, football tournaments, conferences, house meetings and all-night prayer meetings. There was a feeling of safeness when the children were visiting with friends or when sleep-overs were arranged. And there were always plenty of children for them to play with, for although it wasn't Fellowship policy for members to have bigger than average families, it was not unusual for there to be six or seven or even more siblings in a single household. A common view in the wider community was that we were trying to outbreed them. Our house was always full of people, laughter, happiness and noise, and on Saturday mornings there would nearly always be an extra couple of hungry mouths at the breakfast table.

As our children grew into their teenage years, there was an abundance of activities for them and for me too. I enjoyed my responsibilities as a youth leader as well as home group leader. I could combine my love for the outdoors and people with my love for God and my growing appreciation of the Bible. I organised outward bound activities for the teenagers and often, late into the evenings, deep in the mountains or in Ireland's idyllic Lake District, we would sing and pray and tell stories, gathered around a camp fire eating toasted marshmallows.

As a family, we were frequently asked to offer hospitality to visiting guests because of our perceived social standing and the practical advantage of owning a big house. This gave us a rare opportunity to meet informally with leaders and their families from various parts of the UK, Ireland and beyond, which added further to our status in the Fellowship. But it also increased my perplexity for, paradoxically, while our relationships with influential people in the network of international fellowships embedded us more deeply into the community, the experiences also made me feel increasingly uneasy. I could see that the aspects of Fellowship life that most grated on me were endemic at every level and in every place.

While we were serving our visiting guests by offering them hospitality, they weren't grateful to us – they simply took our generosity for granted. They showed no gratitude because it was expected of us, something we had to do. As they saw it, we were privileged to have them in our home.

I was unaware of a hierarchy in those early days, with the result that my practical jokes tended to backfire. There was a party of Germans in my home one Saturday evening, and as we were dishing out the teas and coffees, I asked one, 'Do you take sugar?' to which he answered 'Nine'. Now it was obvious that he meant 'No'; nevertheless, he got nine teaspoons of sugar. It was one of those things I had always wanted to do, but he wasn't even slightly amused. In fact, he was rude, not necessarily because he lacked a sense of humour, which he probably did, but because it wasn't the done thing for people such as I – at the bottom of the pile – to play pranks on the senior leadership, people I was serving because of their elevated position. I had a lot to learn about what was expected of me in regard to hierarchies and submission to authority.

The leaders had so much in common that it was scary. They all read the same books by the same narrow range of writers, and sang the same hymns, to the same tunes. They all venerated the same senior leadership, and they all either ran, or were senior members of, churches that thrived on submission to authority. And they all – me included – had this habit of tilting their heads to the side and making a funny little 'Mmmmm' noise as they prayed.

Over tea, stories would often emerge of difficulties they were having with some of their members. If a shepherd was in business and needed additional employees, the sheep would be expected to make themselves available for work. One young lady I knew had graduated from university, yet she ended up working in her shepherd's restaurant, regardless of the fact that she could easily have found a much better job. And that was the norm.

On one occasion, one of the visiting leaders was furious that a man in his fellowship refused to wind up his own successful business in order to work on a commission-only basis, selling life insurance in his shepherd's company, which was described as a 'kingdom business'. The leader felt that the young business executive had a 'bad attitude to authority' and needed to learn to submit to his shepherd. He was subjected to sustained counselling and prayer, and the teaching of the fathers of the shepherding movement was drummed into him: 'Christians are more vulnerable to demonic attack if they are not under the covering of one in authority over them.' The implied threat was that if he insisted on running his own business, it would collapse. In the end, the young man refused to close his profitable company. But his obstinacy cost him his credibility: he was branded a rebel and marginalised to such an extent that the only honourable option he felt he had was to leave the church – which he did in due course.

The shepherding movement began life in the 1970s following the Neo-Pentecostal charismatic renewal in the late 1950s and early 1960s. The shepherds of Fort Lauderdale, or the 'Fort Lauderdale Five', were concerned that the growing numbers of believers were without structure. They believed that they could introduce a form of leadership that would strengthen the church worldwide, enabling it to cope with the growth in membership. As they saw it, the church was not equipped to nurture the new converts, many of whom were drifting out of the church through lack of pastoral care.

Young Christians need to be discipled, and it was thought that this could only be achieved by their submitting to the authority of a mentor: a mature Christian who would act as a personal pastor for the young Christian. But by the early 1980s there was a growing realisation within the upper echelons of the shepherding movement that the excesses of some of the shepherds and the abuses of power in general had damaged thousands of lives and contributed to the destruction of many marriages.

Shepherding as a concept had burgeoned because it was almost right. It's obvious that a new Christian can benefit enormously by adopting a respectful, deferential attitude to more mature Christians. Indeed, Peter said exactly that as the first century church grew, 'You younger men, accept the authority of the elders' (1 Pet. 5:5), but there's an important and subtle distinction between the Bible model and that promoted by the shepherding movement. Peter taught the concept of young people respecting their elders in general, and this respect was to be given to those who had accumulated wisdom over the years – it was nothing to do with delegated authority or a chain of command.

Not only had the Fort Lauderdale Five overlooked this, they had also overlooked the inherent dangers in the unbiblical concept of one individual being in submission to another exclusively. This was never Peter's intention and it created the opportunity for the strong, who were not necessarily the spiritually mature, to exploit the weak, who weren't necessarily the spiritually immature. As Derek Prince, one of the Fort Lauderdale Five, observed at a more mature stage in his ministry, 'I believe that God ordained the shepherding movement, but the response of some people was very carnal . . . Ultimately, self ambition destroyed it.'[1]

In Stephen Mansfield's book, Derek recalls a comment made by his wife, Lydia, shortly before she died. He said, 'She turned to a friend with whom she had been discussing shepherding and said, almost in tears, "They've got my Derek."'[2]

A constant stream of books and audio tapes from the Fort Lauderdale Five promoted their ideology and, specifically, what they referred to as a vital principle: 'Our attitude toward those whom God sets in delegated authority over us is the outward and visible expression of our attitude toward God himself.'[3] They went further by stressing that, as Christians, 'we do not obey those in authority over us because they are right; we obey them because they are in authority over us.'[4] In other words, it was beyond the remit of a mere sheep to make a judgement as to the correctness or otherwise of an instruction: 'Ours not to reason why, ours but to do and die.'

Even as a young Christian, I could see the danger in this teaching. If we blindly obey those in authority over us we may sin, for they could be wrong. But we were taught that the sheep were not to concern themselves with such matters. In such circumstances, the sin would be 'covered' by the shepherd, because the sheep was obeying God's delegated authority figure. It seemed theologically indefensible to me that anyone other than Jesus, our High Priest, could cover the sins of his people, and so at every available opportunity I would raise the topic with almost every leader to whom we gave hospitality, and some more besides. But every time, unhappy and unconvinced as I was, my conclusion was the same: it would be arrogant in the extreme for me even to begin to think that I could be right and these esteemed gentlemen wrong.

Frequently, however, I was able to put my concerns aside. Music was an important part of our family life. I played guitar, and we'd often have mad jamming sessions at home in the evenings when we could amass a credible mini-orchestra including drums, guitar, violin, harmonica, a didgeridoo and a bodhrán. Music was a major element of Fellowship life too, and my children, being able musicians, loved every minute of it. All the difficulties that were creating anxiety for me went straight over their heads: they didn't even register with them.

Membership of the Fellowship offered many benefits, which when set beside its negative aspects, sometimes made me feel that I should stop moaning and get on with it. My father used to say, 'There's no such thing as a perfect church. If you ever find one, don't go near it! You'll ruin it!' And he was right, but did that mean we turn a blind eye to everything on the basis that every church is made up of imperfect Christians? Where was the line to be drawn? Was there a line to be drawn?

It didn't seem right to me that we were encouraged to believe that we had a monopoly on the truth. What grounds did we have for thinking that? Were Christians who were not part of our stream of things really second-class Christians? – 'our stream of things' being this international network of related fellowships with their governmental chain of command stretching back to the Fort Lauderdale Five.

This superior attitude was demonstrated in a comment made one evening at our home group. A piece of coal fell out of the burning fire and quickly began to lose its brightness on the hearth, and an old sage muttered, 'Oh dear, someone has just left the Fellowship!' It didn't matter that they might have joined another church; the perception was that since they had left the Fellowship they were already growing cold, settling for second best.

Joe was a long-standing member of the Fellowship who often deputised for the leaders when they were off on preaching tours or leaders' conferences. While Tom was giving attention to his international ministry in Hungary or Germany on one occasion, Joe's brief was to reinforce the principle of sheep submitting to their shepherd's authority, so he called a meeting of the men one evening with that specific purpose in mind. Submission was to be demonstrated by regular acts of service, and he illustrated some ways in which the sheep were expected to do this. For example, on Saturday mornings a shepherd was entitled to expect his garden to be populated by his personal flock of sheep, all eagerly mowing, weeding, digging, clipping and tidying so Mr Shepherd could sit in his study resting in the Spirit or reading his newspaper. Mrs Shepherd would be happily serving coffee or cold drinks while Mrs Sheep would be doing the ironing, cleaning, shopping and childminding.

As Joe preached that night, we could sense that there was a new intensity in the atmosphere, with a more demanding level of commitment and accountability being called for. He painted a word picture: 'It's a Thursday evening. You and your wife are about to set off to a quiet restaurant for a meal with some friends. The phone rings. It's your shepherd calling to tell you that he had planned an evening out too, but his baby-sitter has let him down. He needs you to step in. If there is ill feeling or hesitation in your attitude,' continued Joe, 'you have a problem with authority. You must gladly offer to baby-sit, even before he asks.' In other words, not only were the plans and ambitions of the sheep to be subject to those of the shepherd, but the wives were also to take second place to the shepherd in the pecking order.

The River of Life Fellowship was obsessed with authority, and that evening was no different. As frequently happened, the New Testament story of the Roman Centurion who came to Jesus seeking healing for his servant was trotted out. In the account in Matthew

8:7–9, Jesus offered to bring his healing to the soldier's home but the soldier resisted, saying, 'Lord, I am not worthy to have you come into my home. Just say the word from where you are, and my servant will be healed! I know, because I am under the authority of my superior officers and I have authority over my soldiers. I only need to say, "Go," and they go, or "Come," and they come.' Joe interpreted this to mean you could only exercise authority if you were under authority, and that it was our Christian duty to exercise authority in the home, in the workplace, in prayer, and over demons. Authority was a key issue.

As usual, Joe's talk was recorded, partly for the dissemination of the teaching to those who for whatever reason had missed the meeting, partly for people to listen to the talk over and over again, and partly, I suspect, for the senior leaders to monitor the speaker. However, one of the men who was present and had bought a tape recording carelessly left it lying around in his bedroom where his mother found it, listened to it, was appalled by it, and promptly ensured that it found its way into the hands of the appropriate individual in the BBC.

Meanwhile, Tom returned from his missionary trip and was immediately confronted by Kevin and me at the head of a very long queue. He had already heard the tape recording and was badly shaken, not because he was remorseful but because he suspected that he was soon to be exposed to an outside world that he believed had no understanding of kingdom principles. It was he who had the inside track to God, and he simply could not see that there could be a divergence between what he wanted and what God wanted.

Kevin and I pressed him, 'Tom, either the contents of that tape are an accurate representation of the beliefs and practices of this outfit – if so, we're out of here.

Alternatively, Joe went over the top – in which case, say so, correct him, state how it really is and the chances are we'll all live happily ever after.'

Tom answered not a word. He was almost catatonic and it became embarrassing. He refused to answer, and however we framed the questions and regardless of how often and from what angle we prodded, he stared transfixed at a spot on the carpet. He was convinced that he was not accountable to anyone apart from those above him in the hierarchy of our group of related fellowships, half a world away on the other side of the Atlantic. Those below him didn't know anything of the ways of God. He had often reinforced his lofty position in God's kingdom by quoting Psalm 103:7 '[God] revealed his character to Moses and his deeds to the people of Israel.' Tom and Moses enjoyed God's confidence, being given an insight into the way God does things, while the people of Israel and the people of the River of Life Fellowship could only see God's deeds. We could only stand on the sidelines and watch.

In due course a full-length television documentary was made and broadcast on Irish TV, laying bare excesses and abuses of power that were obvious. The results could have been, perhaps should have been, catastrophic, but they weren't. The official line was 'Babylon is at the door.' David Koresh used a similar tactic to maintain his support before the massacre in Waco, Texas. We were told 'This is the work of the enemy, the outsiders who don't understand us. We must stick together,' and to a degree we did.

We, as a family, should have cut our ties with the Fellowship then, but we didn't. No one did, despite all the grumbling and discontent. When his position was threatened, as it was then, Tom would go to great lengths to remind us that he had foregone a lucrative professional career and had forsaken and had been forsaken by friends and family to follow the Spirit's leading for our benefit. Whether or not that was true, we didn't know, but we simply could not abandon our suffering pastor who had sacrificed so much for us. Leaving was not an option.

We didn't leave then, but the episode had planted another doubt in my head that led to an escapade that would further expose the leaders' tactics. I knew that God understood my reluctance to embrace what was expected of the sheep, to obey without question the teachings and practices of the River of Life Fellowship. Clearly there was a problem, and while I was quite prepared to accept that the problem might be me, I wasn't sure. Frequently I would reflect over my former life of debauchery and the conclusion was always the same: these men were praying through the night, often for me, as I lay with someone else's wife or in a drunken stupor. How could I question their integrity? How could I be right and they wrong?

I needed guidance, but I felt that, given my background, I couldn't trust my own judgement. Nor could I expect my shepherd to provide an objective insight, however well-intentioned he might be. The only one I could trust here was God, so I would ask God what I should do. I would pray and fast, and he would show me the truth. It was that simple, and I began my time of prayer and fasting with a wonderful feeling of freshness and expectancy. It was like having my dedicated hotline to God. I needed direction, I asked him to lead me, and he would show me the way. And I felt a little lift of excitement, for soon the uncertainty that had dogged me, held me back from throwing myself into full and unfettered participation in the activities of the Fellowship, would be gone. Either that, or it would be confirmed and we would move on.

I casually mentioned to my shepherd that I had decided to pray and fast for two weeks as I sought God's
guidance on a matter that was concerning me. 'What's
concerning you?' he asked. When I told him, I thought he
was about to go into orbit. 'Such audacity! How dare you!'
– And I was wheeled off to be straightened out by Tom.

My overwhelming feeling as I was systematically
stripped down by the two of them was one of utter frustration. Only a couple of years previously I had neither
time nor room for God in my life, and these guys were
so unhappy about my lifestyle that I was frequently on
their prayer agenda. In those earlier days, the very suggestion of me making myself accountable to anyone
apart from my bank manager would have been quite
unthinkable. Now, all I wanted was to hear from God
and they were still not satisfied. What was the problem?

This was the problem: 'Your shepherd is God's
spokesman in your life. You cannot be trusted to hear
God's voice. Satan may whisper in your ear and you
don't have the spiritual maturity to distinguish his voice
from God's.'

That struck me as odd. In addition, and in my view the
real issue, they saw it as a calculated insult for me to go
over my shepherd's head direct to God. I had intended
no such insult. I had grown to love God and I trusted
him. Sure, he was my shepherd's God, but he was my
God too, and anyway, I wasn't convinced about this
'chain of command' thing. If I asked God a question from
a sincere and open heart, he would find a way to speak
to me. And, spiritually immature as I was, the words of
John 10: 4–5 sprang into my mind: 'After he [the Good
Shepherd] has gathered his own flock, he walks ahead of
them, and they follow him because they recognize his
voice. They won't follow a stranger; they will run from
him because they don't recognize his voice.'

I believed that God was speaking to me from his word right there, and so I repeated it, and their faces turned a funny purpleish colour as I watched them wince in unison.

'Who do you think you are? How dare you question the very foundation on which the shepherding movement is built? Have you forgotten what you were before you became a member here? Is that the extent of your gratitude? Where do you think you would be now if God had not used us to rescue you? There are benefits to belonging here, Adam, but there are responsibilities too. You can't have one without the other!'

But what about grace, I thought? What about God's undeserved goodness and provision for me? And then another couple of scriptures came to mind: the story of the man, blind from birth whom Jesus had healed. Because the Pharisees hated Jesus, they were interrogating the ex-blind man, to see if they could find a way to discredit Jesus. They said, 'We know God spoke to Moses, as for this man, we don't know anything about him' (Jn. 9:29).

The man answered, 'Why, that's very strange! . . . He healed my eyes, and yet you don't know anything about him! Well, God doesn't listen to sinners, but he is ready to hear those who worship him and do his will. Never since the world began, has anyone been able to open the eyes of someone born blind. If this man were not from God, he couldn't do it' (Jn. 9:30–33).

The Pharisees were stumped, so they exploded. 'You were born in sin! . . . Are you trying to teach us?' And they threw him out of the synagogue (Jn. 9:34). I reminded my Pharisees of that, too. In my simplicity, I suggested that their reaction had a certain resonance with that text, and I thought both would have a stroke at any moment. But my heart was pristine, it really was, and I felt so misunderstood that I cried. I actually broke down and I cried in sheer frustration at their blindness and stubborn refusal even to try to see things from my point of view. To them, I was wrong, they were right. The matter was closed.

But I began to think that perhaps I was ungrateful and arrogant to have asked God what I could have asked my shepherd. Maybe these were good men against whom I was harbouring a proud, rebellious spirit. Perhaps God had indeed brought them into my life to rescue me from depravity. They had saved my marriage. They had probably saved my life. They were right – I was wrong, and I was so disheartened that I didn't even finish my time of fasting. I simply submitted once more in the mistaken belief that God required of me what they required: conformity and a degree of obedience that would crush my free spirit. They kept me in my place by reminding me, sometimes subtly, sometimes brutally, that just as God had used them to bring me into his kingdom, so he would use them to keep me there.

# CHAPTER 2

# MY SLIDE TO THE PERIPHERY

My general unhappiness, compounded by the impression that I was the only person in the entire Fellowship who was complaining, began to create tension in my home. I was certainly the only member of my family who was troubled; everyone else was happier than they had ever been and they saw my continual moaning as a threat to their secure future. We fell out over silly things, usually, such as the early morning prayer meetings that were held during the week. I have always hated mornings. Like Garfield the cat, I wouldn't mind so much if they started later. Daphne and I agreed that we would go on alternate mornings – no, the truth is that she agreed that we would go alternate mornings. Given my innate distaste for morning activities, I would never commit myself to a meeting for any purpose at seven o'clock in the morning, three times a week. So when it was my turn, we argued: almost invariably, I would opt for the blankets. Who ever heard of husband and wife arguing about a prayer meeting!

While at times I felt that everything was wrong about me, the root of the malaise was deeper. I was a young Christian, disgusted with the way I had lived most of my life to that point, and I was simply trying to live as I knew I should. But however hard I tried, I was always made to feel second rate, that I was damaged goods. For example, I found it difficult to stop smoking, and in my part of the world smoking is seen as worldly and sinful. But rather than acceptance, support and a smidgen of understanding, I would be compared to others. 'Why can't you be like Tony? He stopped smoking immediately when he became a Christian. What's the matter with you?' I even asked for prayer to stiffen my resolve but I was addicted to nicotine and it would take time. In fact, it took several years.

But there was another side to it. One chap felt that my smoking was a demonic issue, and had recently been taught that when you cast out demons, you have to tell them where to go. It's not good enough to say, 'Out in Jesus' name!' You must specify a destination. Unfortunately, my sense of humour got the better of me as Dave instructed the spirits to 'Get thee hence into Bangor Bay!' Sitting with my eyes closed, I pictured dozens of little sun-tanned nicotine demons with little swim suits and bathing hats on, meekly obeying Dave the Deliverer. And, of course, when I chuckled during a session of exorcism, I was deemed to be all but beyond hope.

In spite of the efforts of my siblings in Christ to slot me beneath them in the spiritual pecking order, and despite the fact that I occasionally agreed with them, I had a deep down feeling that my cigarette consumption, my unruly sense of humour and all the other things about me that I didn't like much and they liked even less, didn't matter to God. I felt like the younger brother in the parable of the Prodigal Son. Father had forgiven, totally and unconditionally, but the older brother wanted blood, and the hierarchical structure of the Fellowship would always support the view that God would never undermine his lieutenants, not even if they were wrong.

There was an occasion when, in my mind's eye, I saw a shepherd on a Judean hillside as he sat in his little hut on a wet, windswept winter's night, warming his toes at his brazier. 'Well,' he was muttering to himself, 'if the sheep need me they know where I am.' Had I needed my shepherd urgently at any time of the day or night, he would have been there for me, I know that. But there was a condition. I was to do all the running. The Fellowship was not based on mutual love and respect but on an unequal distribution of power. Yes, they were available to help me but only on the condition that I humbled myself and acknowledged their superiority.

A senior manager in a commercial organisation may boast that he is accessible to his staff, and indeed he may be, but it would be considered unconventional, if not unprofessional, if he were to take the initiative in caring for his junior staff. So it was in the shepherding movement: for all the rhetoric about commitment, covenant relationships and caring for the flock, there seemed to be a general lack of awareness that when a person most needs love and company and friendship, a shoulder to cry on, that's often the time when they're least likely to ask for help. Or perhaps as in Jesus' parable of the ninety-nine sheep, (Mt. 18:12,13) the little lost lamb may be trapped in a bush and can't move.

I was becoming increasingly unhappy with the credibility gap I saw in the River of Life Fellowship, but probably because most of my wife's and my children's friends and social contacts were centred there, I compromised and retreated to the fringes. Apart from leading some children's work and taking responsibility for a home group, I restricted my active involvement to occasional guerrilla attacks when the absurdity of it all got too much for me. I would lob a playful hand grenade in the form of an awkward question or an observation from Scripture that I knew didn't sit well with the direction of a discussion in one of the leaders' meetings, to which I was occasionally invited.

On the thorny topic of Sabbath observance or abstinence from alcohol, Colossians 2:16 would never fail to ruffle feathers: 'Don't let anyone condemn you for what you eat or drink, or for not celebrating . . . Sabbaths.' I never argued that everyone is free to interpret Scripture in a way that suits their chosen lifestyle, but I would always have pressed for the freedom to be guided by the Spirit of Truth, rather than being restricted to a dogma imposed from above.

So defensive were the leadership that those who were wont to ask awkward questions were consigned to irrelevance by the figurative pinning of a 'Rebel' badge on their breast. The term would be used teasingly, even with an appearance of affection at first, but it was extremely effective. Those who were not predisposed to be rebellious or given to asking searching questions would withdraw. The genuine article, however, persisted and the label stuck. And it could be very subtle. If a recognised rebel were to raise a difficult topic at a meeting, you'd see heads dropping to avoid eye contact. Mocking smirks would appear, accompanied by a stony silence. All but the strong and determined would retreat in embarrassment, for the wearer of the 'Rebel' badge had become the problem, while the real problem, to which, while he was trying to draw attention, was ignored.

On one occasion, the accounts were being made public, as public as they ever were. This is often another symptom of an abusive church, where the view 'It's none of your business what we do with the money God tells you to give us!' seems to be the norm. Many of us wondered why the secrecy was necessary. None of the full-time elders' salaries or other benefits were ever shown. All the salaries and expenses were lumped together, appearing in the accounts as a single figure under one heading. I stood to my feet, opened my mouth and uttered only a half a syllable, when Alan the Administrator, the 'financial elder' who knew what was coming, sought to aim his spotlight on my 'Rebel' badge by trotting out the standard justification, 'This is an agreed practice in all the other fellowships within our stream of things, and blah, blah, blah . . .' But the meeting disintegrated into peals of uncontrollable of laughter when I responded, 'Alan, might it be an idea for me to ask the question before you answer it, please?'

I was in an odd position. Remaining on the periphery where I was happiest, I was like a backbencher in Parliament; I had no party line to tow and could speak freely, while offering a degree of general support. But for a variety of reasons that I've already touched on, I was seen as a significant member. That was the term they liked to use, partly because of my perceived social status, and partly because of my silver hair. Although only in my forties, I was one of a handful of relative oldies.

My free-thinking disposition and my interest in outdoor activities – fishing, shooting, mountaineering and the like – led to a group of younger men of like minds gravitating around me. Informally, we would meet two or three times a month to discuss the relevance of our faith in the real world. Never one for holy huddles, the earthiness of my approach attracted them, and it was mutual. Often we would spend weekends camping among the mountains and lakes simply having fun, but this unnerved the elders. They couldn't get a handle on me, and as a result they couldn't rein in the group of young men whose company I enjoyed so much. I was a loose cannon.

Then one day the phone rang. It was Tom. He wanted to see me. After ten years' fairly faithful, if abrasive, service – at least I was consistent – the time had come for me to enter the inner sanctum. I was to become an accredited shepherd. My initial reaction was one of surprise – not so much at the offer, but at the mixed bag of emotions that surfaced from God alone knows where. At one level it would be a pleasant change to feel accepted. I could hang up my 'Rebel' badge, and would finally be taken seriously. It would be good to be valued and trusted, someone who could contribute positively to the efficient operation of part of the body of Christ – all I ever really wanted. I was still struggling with issues of shepherding, serving and enforced tithing, but now people would be serving me. I could set aside my concerns for the greater good.

The cadre of young men who formed my unofficial home group would be pleased to have a proper shepherd, rather than some renegade, John the Baptist type, always in the middle of controversy, forever asking awkward questions. My wife was also delighted at the increase in status being offered me. Most people had considered the relationship between her and Tom's wife to be unequal. Perhaps it offended their competitive sensibilities: the wives of sheep should socialise at their own level. And the children were happy too, for in the same way it was irregular for the children of sheep, lambs I suppose, to be found playing with the children of the shepherds.

However, after two or three days of turmoil and prayer, I decided I simply could not bring myself to accept the proffered promotion. I would be completely compromising myself. Here was a paradox I could see right through and yet was being tempted to overlook. I was being offered authority in the hope that it would keep me quiet. The serial dissenter was being invited into the place where he could be controlled, where he would be expected to tow the party line. I could picture the scenario. 'You're now a shepherd. This is what's expected of you. Do you want to be a sheep again?' So the decision was made; not only would I refuse a place in the cloisters of power, but I would leave the River of Life Fellowship and take my family with me.

Was this an overreaction? I think not, although that was my family's view at first. But as we talked it through, there was a level of agreement. What sort of people were these? Here was an organisation that would stop at nothing to get its way, to control the uncontrollable, to twist and squirm and manipulate. Rather than listen to what was being said by people with the ability to think outside the box and then evaluate it, the dissident was either gagged, humiliated or silenced by whatever means available. These were not the methods of God's kingdom, nor did they reflect its principles. They were just the power-struggles I was familiar with in the business world – and I wanted no part of them.

A shockwave reverberated through the leadership when I announced I would be leaving. There had been a major split seven years earlier that resulted in the birth of another church – Belfast Christian Trust. Another split might do irreparable damage, and so there was a flurry of activity aimed at doing whatever had to be done to keep me on board.

The previous split had taken place shortly after Derek Prince renounced the shepherding movement and publicly apologised for his part in the damage that had been done. That was in 1983, but Tom, closely associated though he was with Derek and the other Fort Lauderdale shepherds, had been unwilling to offer more than an explanation when things went wrong. An

apology would have more helpful in rebuilding damaged lives, but Tom was unable to make the radical and
decisive steps that were needed to redress the iniquities
of the past. His approach, as always, was of the 'Ignore
it and it will go away' variety, and so half the leadership
of the River of Life Fellowship left, taking their flock
with them.

Strangely, it never occurred to me to move out at this
time. This was partly because the structure of the
Fellowship was such that it was almost two communities under the one roof. Often you would hear people
say, 'Are you on Tom's or Daniel's side?' I was on Tom's
side. And at this point only a few very senior people
were aware that a split had been in the making for perhaps a year or more, Derek's departure was the catalyst
and not the instigation.

So in an attempt to placate me, Tom seemed prepared
to meet my major objections, even offering to drop
tithing and submission to a specific shepherd as conditions for membership. Such was his fear that the dribble
of members leaving would become a haemorrhage.

A number of people from within and without the River
of Life Fellowship had approached me around this time,
suggesting that I should start a new church. I even had a
'prophetic word' from a dear friend who sold his house in
a nearby town and relocated to be part of my new community. But there were over sixty churches in our town,
which had a population of less than eighty thousand
souls. We needed another church like we needed a hole in
the head. To start yet another in a grossly over-churched
community would send out only one message: 'You're all
out of step apart from me. Stand back and I'll show you
how it's done.'

Our town didn't need more churches. Rather, we
needed more people who were prepared to be Jesus to

their neighbours, to visit the sick and those in prison; prepared to be engaged in the world, fully involved and yet untarnished by it. It needed people who were different, but not aloof. True Christianity is more than mere church attendance, for while it is true that a good church provides teaching, fellowship and emotional support, at the heart of Christian service is the word 'Go!', not 'Settle'. And while it may be an overstatement to say that true Christianity leaves insufficient time for church services, it would certainly rule out most of the multiplying meetings we had in the River of Life Fellowship.

Why were there so many meetings? At one stage I counted thirteen meetings in a typical week, all of which the dedicated member was expected to attend. The purpose was to create our own 'spiritual social whirl'. The busier we were kept, the less likely we would be to engage in meaningful activities outside the orb of the Fellowship. And so our lives became increasingly bound up in Fellowship activities that separated us from the real world in which it was normal to ask questions. In such circumstances, you can lose touch with reality; the weird can become the norm.

There were other reasons why I wasn't interested in developing a new church. I'd had enough of these tiny fractious little groups, made up of people who believed they were God's gift to Ireland. And I didn't want sheep crawling all over my garden on a Saturday morning. If my wife needed extra help with household chores, our children and I would shoulder the burden, or we would pay for someone to help in the home. And if the gardening got too much for us, we'd hire a gardener or cover the thing with tarmac. I certainly wasn't into discipling people by grounding them into a culture of subservience. For me, true discipling has more to do with serving those who are less spiritually mature. A leader is a person whom others want to follow, not one who drives and dictates.

I had been part of the shepherding movement for eleven years. Questions about the integrity of the senior man had arisen within a week of my joining, and my first serious misgivings began only two years after becoming a member, so what had kept me there for another nine? And why is it that many of those who appeared to be as unhappy as I was then, remain there until this day?

It's true that misery loves company, and some people prefer to remain where they are unhappy and unfulfilled. In a perverted way, they have more in common with each other than they have with other Christians in a more traditional Christian environment; they understand each other better. So for an individual to move out of the Fellowship into unfamiliar surroundings in which they might be asked to explain their part in a Christian community that was viewed as odd, is the least preferred option, a frightening prospect.

And of course there was always the nagging doubt that the leaders who presented themselves as super spiritual beings – and who were seen as such – might have grasped some mystical truth that eluded us lesser mortals. Compared to them, I believed I was spiritually immature, but I desperately wanted to please God and they appeared to know how to please God. However, because they had succeeded in presenting themselves as God's intermediaries – that was at the heart of the shepherding movement – I mistook their acceptance as God's acceptance and, as a consequence, I saw their rejection as God's rejection.

However, the time had come when I simply could no longer swallow the closely held and rigidly enforced principles of shepherding, servitude and tithing, and I had a growing sense that God didn't approve of them either. But since shepherding, servitude and tithing were among the basic elements of membership of the River of Life Fellowship, my difficulty with them was not something that could easily be ignored.

Like many who join what the sociologists call New Religious Movements (NRMs), I had joined the Fellowship partly because I found traditional religion dull, boring and hypocritical. (I still do.) As a member of a traditional denomination, it would be difficult for me to be anything other than an insignificant cog in a vast and impersonal machine. I had thought there might have been a role for me in bringing the Kingdom of Heaven to earth, and that the River of Life Fellowship was God's chosen vehicle. Indeed, part of our teaching was that a thick black cloud of demonic power was stretched over our town like some great evil tarpaulin. We actually believed that our praises punched holes in it to allow the power and blessing of God to pierce through and flood our streets – where on earth did that come from? – when the prayers and praises of generations of faithful servants were alleged to have failed.

At a more mundane level, the attraction was that I could belong to a friendly community of like-minded people, sharing values that I could not see in secular society. My social life and that of my family were rooted in the many activities there but what was it that held me for so long, in spite of my multiplying doubts? There was always the niggling feeling that the elders knew the Bible better than I did, and had a more intimate relationship with God than I had. Another reason may have been intellectual and spiritual inertia, a resistance to change, or to put it another way, better the devil you know than the devil you don't.

However, without doubt, the most significant factor behind my reluctance to leave was the fear of living in an unprotected state outside of the covering. The idea that a Christian community has the capacity to offer a protective covering, outside of which the 'unsubmitted' Christian is more easily picked off by the devil, was widely accepted in the shepherding movement. It must rank among the meanest and most subtle of all deceptions that minimise God's ability and commitment to shepherd his own. It is also idolatrous in that it places men in a position where only God has the right to be, but it is a most effective means by which free-spirited people are rendered powerless and nailed to the pew.

Dr Ken Blue, in his classic *Healing Spiritual Abuse*[5] states:

> Spiritual abusers are curiously naïve about the effects of their exploitation. They rarely intend to hurt their victims. They are usually so narcissistic, or so focused on some great thing they are doing for God, that they don't notice the wounds they are inflicting on their followers. So though I maintain that spiritual abuse is evil and dangerous and must be stopped, my definition of it leaves out the term intent to hurt.

Ken and I have discussed our respective experiences and I go along with him, but only to a point. For years, all I could see was my hurt, my pain, and I grieved that there was never a hint of remorse, no apology to the many, many folks who had been damaged, some of them permanently. There was no opportunity for closure.

One professional man whom I know well is still on medication and unable to hold down a responsible job, twelve years after leaving the River of Life Fellowship, such was the extent of psychological damage inflicted on him. Therefore, while I would not accuse any of the leaders whom I knew of a deliberate and calculated attempt to inflict damage, the fact remains, deep and lasting hurts were caused. And I am convinced that most of the leaders knew the pain and stress their leadership was inflicting. Perhaps they thought it was a price that had to be paid for spiritual growth.

# CHAPTER 3

# OBSTACLES TO FREEDOM

Tom's initial reaction when I declared that my days as a member of the River of Life Fellowship were numbered, was the comment, 'Your pastoral ministry is on the line here, Adam!' To which I replied, 'Tom, if God has called me to a pastoral ministry, not even you can defrock me. And if he hasn't, I don't want one.' The scramble for power didn't impress me: indeed, I found it embarrassing to be called 'shepherd' or 'pastor'. It happened once as I visited a friend in prison. My friend's quota of visits had been used up and I managed to arrange another as a representative of his church: my first and last ecclesiastical visit. 'Would Pastor Harbinson please come to the visiting room!' boomed out over the intercom – not for me! And I simply could not contemplate a bunch of lads forming an orderly queue to bow and scrape before me as they handed me their tithes each month.

There followed many meetings between Tom and me. I was trying hard not to create a fuss; I just wanted to leave, and I was becoming increasingly intrigued by the big deal Tom appeared to be turning it into. Why did I want to leave? Where was I going? How long had I been unhappy? What in particular was upsetting me?

For me, all the talking had been done. I had a deep and settled knowing that there was no turning back. In any case, there was no single issue. Rather, there was an accumulation of factors, a build-up that had taken place over a period of years. A number of people approached me unofficially with the suggestion, 'Give it another shot: after all, we've been down some hard roads together.' And yes, we had been along some hard roads, and yes, it did sound tempting, but I suspected a hidden agenda, an underlying plan to weaken my resolve. If I could be persuaded to stay, I know it would have been almost impossible for me to make the move at some point in the future. And it wasn't that I longed to be part of another church, although the one that we did attach ourselves to for a while after we left the Fellowship did beckon.

Tom said he would like to speak to Daphne, and I saw no reason no object. I had no problem with him meeting with the pair of us, but he didn't mean the pair of us: he wanted to see her alone, and that was a different matter. We both sensed a classic attempt to divide and conquer, and so I refused. But he genuinely could not understand why someone whom he had been influential in bringing to faith wanted to move on. And so I'm sure that to some extent the meetings were his attempt to understand why I was leaving the safety of his fold, for in his world people didn't move on, they shrank from change, they were content to go round and round in irrelevant, pious little eddies, always doing but not getting anywhere.

Tom was right in his belief that the River of Life Fellowship offered everything any sedentary Christian could ever want. There was an abundance of teaching to be had: a solid hour every Sunday morning and more on most Sunday evenings, with another couple of blasts during the week. The praise and worship were good by most standards, the sense of community was real, and now with the addition of a Christian school, how could anyone want more? But that misses the point. The Christian life is a journey, it's not a picnic in the park, however well tended the gardens. The Great Commission is to 'Go into all the world and preach the Good News to everyone, everywhere' (Mk.16:15), not 'find a cosy corner somewhere and relax'. Christians are intended to be a nomadic tribe.

Tom's bewilderment spilled out all over our meetings. At one stage, there was even a touch of emotion, something I had never seen in all the years I had known him. 'How can you do this to me? You're my friends!' I could sense that Daphne was wavering under the intense emotional pressure. I assured him, 'Yes, Tom, we are your friends, but we're leaving your church.' And at that point a little light went on in my head. Tom was taking it personally because it was *his* church.

Then he tried the threatening tack. About a year earlier we had removed Jonny, our then eight-year-old son who has learning difficulties, from the state education system, in the hope that he would benefit from the more pastoral, lower teacher/pupil ratio in the primary school that was part of the Fellowship. And it was indeed to his benefit, although it hurt my pocket. However, while the official line was that all and any were welcome to attend the school – indeed part of its role was evangelism in the community – the reaction now was, 'I'm not sure it would be a good idea for Jonathan to stay at our school if you're no longer to be part of the River of Life Fellowship.' This was clearly a last-ditch attempt to whip us back into line.

Tom asked if I would agree to a meeting with all the elders, presumably to see if they could succeed where he had failed, to find out why we were going or if they could persuade me to stay. I was beginning to feel impatient. I just wanted to go but I agreed to meet with them, and again we went round and round in ever decreasing circles, not making any sense, until finally I felt the Lord saying to me, 'The time for talking is over. Just go!' And I said so.

It's strange how, when an individual or a group goes to great lengths to proclaim who and what they are or are not, quite often the opposite is true. Tom often said, 'We are not a cult. Cults are easy to get into and hard to get out of.' It's true that there was a 'Seekers Course' for those who showed an interest in joining, in order to unpack the beliefs and practices of the River of Life Fellowship. The course, a series of evening teaching sessions, was ostensibly a filter, acting as a barrier to any who might not be one of the chosen few with the necessary degree of commitment. In reality, in all the years I was there, while many lost interest or didn't have a genuine interest in the first place, I was not aware of anyone being filtered out.

Clearly, the River of Life Fellowship was not difficult to join. And was it easy to get out of? Well, the hoops I was being asked to jump through, the insinuation that I'd die 'out there', the emotional blackmail and the relentless persuasion had only one purpose – to make life outside of the Fellowship appear anything but safe. The pressure to stay was enormous.

Finally, when all else failed, the ultimate weapon was deployed. 'Adam, this is of the devil.' For the first time, I had a sharp intake of breath. I hesitated. A swirl of memories engulfed my mind and once again I could see myself in my depravity while these good men were organising all night prayer meetings, praise services, Bible study classes and weeks of prayer and fasting to usher in God's kingdom. And, predictably, the ubiquitous concept of the 'covering' presented itself to me yet again in a most fearsome way. Maybe I was safe here. Who did I think I was? If this place was good enough for all these fine upstanding men, what was my problem? Daphne used to pour scorn on some of my ambitions and plans, saying, 'Why can't you be an ordinary Christian?' At times I agreed. Why not indeed?

I began to wonder why it is that spiritual abusers thrive on making others feel dirty, just as the Pharisees did in their day. My Father whispered in my ear, 'I have loved you . . . with an everlasting love' (Jer. 31:3). He told me, 'Your sins and lawless acts I will remember no more' (Heb. 10:17). Yet in the Fellowship I was constantly reminded of who and what I was before I was rescued, and how gracious and tolerant my brothers had been in welcoming me into the fold while the stench of sin still clung to my clothes like stale vomit.

My Father would never do that. He says, 'He has removed our rebellious acts as far away from us as the east is from the west' (Ps. 103:12). That's the God I wanted to worship and serve, but I didn't see too much of him around the River of Life Fellowship.

As I teetered on the fence for those few seconds and gazed deep into Tom's eyes, almost audibly I could hear my Father, my Good Shepherd say, 'Son, I've spoken clearly. Don't you trust me?'

'No Tom, it's not of the devil. It's of God, and we're going.' And go we did.

# CHAPTER 4

# THE BACKLASH

Men never do evil so completely and cheerfully as when
they do it from a religious conviction.

Blaise Pascal

The elders who ruled by fear were now driven by fear.
There had been a number of occasions in my decade-
long membership of the River of Life Fellowship when I
teetered on the edge of freedom. Ironically, although I
had come to regard the community as my family, it was
fear of rejection, not love and acceptance, that kept me
there. On some of those occasions when I thought I
should leave and become part of a 'proper' church, I
would dream in the night that I had deserted the
Fellowship, and I'd wake up in a cold sweat. What if
these people really are a faithful remnant in a rebellious
and decadent world? If I turn my back on them, am I
turning my back on God too? Will God reject me if I
reject them? And what about the 'covering' upon which
such emphasis was laid? – and once again I would submit.

But this time it was different. I had finally woken up
to what was going on, and with the fog of confusion

now clearing, I had a new confidence in my relationship with God. The leaders of the community that was once my spiritual home had been subtly exploiting the authority I had yielded to them. They would say, 'My role is to press you into Jesus,' and I tried to believe them, truly I did, but in reality they had been doing quite the opposite. They saw their authority as being delegated to them in a chain of command that stretched, like a military hierarchy, all the way back to God. I was expected to be subservient to them but there was neither engagement nor intimacy. Ours had been a cold and wooden relationship.

They faced a major dilemma. Since the Harbinsons were seen as a significant family, it was always going to be difficult for us to slip out unnoticed – by far the pre-ferred option of the leadership. Tom, fearful of a high-profile exodus, said to me, 'If you leave now you'll start a ball rolling, and who knows where it will end?' He was concerned that our leaving would precipitate the crum-bling of ivory towers. Whether I was right or wrong was never the issue. Our leaving might constitute a threat to the elders' position of unquestioned authority, and now that I was flatly rejecting that authority and their exclu-sive right to speak God's word into my life, the gloves came off.

To a man, the leaders were seriously rattled, and with every failure to threaten, cajole, manipulate or frighten me back under their authority, they became more frantic in their zeal for self-preservation. It was open war. As they saw it, they were fighting for their survival, but rather than dealing with real issues, the leaders were committed to the maintenance of the status quo at any price.

There was an undercurrent of discontent at the time that served to intensify their fears, which were exacerbated by the rumours that I was intent on setting up a rival church. As we have seen, a handful of men had approached me saying that if I had such intentions, they would be among the first to join me – but I had no such plans.

The leaders were determined that we couldn't be seen to leave over doctrinal issues. If I disagreed with their teaching, left and was seen to survive – or even prosper – then their doctrine of the protective covering would be in shreds. The belief that there was no real spiritual life outside the shepherding movement had to be protected at all costs.

So the dilemma was this: on the one hand, if the Harbinson clan could not be persuaded to stay, damage limitation demanded that we slide off the radar screen with nobody saying anything – unlikely. The other option was for a story to emerge that would prove there was no real theological disagreement between us. Someone had to come up with something that would convince the remaining watchful membership that I had a hidden agenda.

Meanwhile, I was asked to offer a public explanation, tactfully of course, of why we were leaving. I agreed to say simply that I felt it was time for us to move on, make a few kind comments about our decade as members, and leave it at that. I realised I was being used but that didn't matter to me. All I wanted was to put the past behind me and to get on with life.

It was a midsummer Sunday evening in 1991 when I last stood in the pulpit of the place I had loved, hated and feared, and from which I was soon to be free. As I surveyed the faces of the hundred or so people whom I thought I knew so well, I felt a new liberty. I looked into the hollow eyes of some of the men who, like me, had so often been on the verge of freedom but had drawn back for lack of courage to think for themselves. Two words

entered my mind – 'spiritually gelded'. Without man-
hood and unable to reproduce – they were truly the pastor's progeny. As I stood behind the lectern that evening,
diplomatically avoiding anything that might threaten an
amicable end to our relationship, I thought that the leaders were happy to let us go graciously, if not with their
blessing. I was wrong.

Things quickly turned nasty. Martin Henshaw and his
wife Rachel had been close friends of ours for years, and
our families got along well together too. Their son was
encouraged to look to me for wisdom and guidance; I
was his spiritual daddy. Martin had always been sup-
portive and open-hearted towards me and the numerous projects I had driven forward over the years. If I was
raising money for a new hospital in Uganda, he would
be first in the queue with a fistful of five-pound notes. If
I was planning to take a bunch of youngsters into the
mountains for a weekend, I could always rely on Martin
to help with the logistics and more. He was always
there, through thick and thin.

There was an occasion when, during a home group
meeting I was leading, Martin and his wife wanted to
bring up some of the inconsistencies that bothered them
about the way things were being run by the leaders of
the River of Life Fellowship. I believed it was inappropriate. It was neither the time nor the place to air views
that risked reducing our meeting to a griping session.
He disagreed and brought the matter to a close by saying that if he could not be free to air his grievances
'. . . then there's no point in me being here' and they
trundled off home.

But another couple who'd been in the group that
evening rang Martin the next day in a demonstration of
solidarity, saying that in their view I had treated him
and his wife in a cavalier fashion. Martin's response

surprised them, but it didn't surprise me when they told me, 'How dare you say that about Adam! He's the leader of our group and deserves our honesty and loyalty!' That was the nature of the man.

A couple of weeks after that fateful Sunday night in June 1991, our two families were on holiday together in Portugal for the third time. The relationship was beginning to fray around the edges. Each evening we'd sit for hours under the stars, chatting about this and that over a glass or six of wine. But the conversation invariably turned to their conviction that we had forsaken the safety of the fold. Even then it struck me as odd when Martin repeatedly asked, 'But why did you really leave?' It seemed he had convinced himself, or had been convinced by others, that I was hiding something. He simply could not understand why anyone would want to leave the church that was everything to him and had been almost everything to me. Things became strained. Not just between our families, but between Martin and Rachel too, and that was ominous.

Things turned an unpleasant corner when we arrived home from our holiday that summer. Martin was a kitchen manufacturer, I was his business/financial advisor. There began a series of meetings at his initiation during which, for the first time, he questioned the integrity of my business dealings. Each time we met I was able to demonstrate that I had always acted in his best interests and that all was above board, as indeed I believed it was. But when he returned again and again, sometimes with less than an hour between our meetings, with more questions and signs of increasing agitation, it was becoming obvious that there was an underlying issue here that wasn't going to go away.

The last such meeting we had was at the end of August, just two months after my departure from the

Fellowship, and I had the feeling that things were fast coming to a head. The conversation went round in circles, until finally Martin asked if I was serious about leaving the Fellowship. It sounded like an ultimatum. 'Is there any chance you'd reconsider?' I said there wasn't, and with tears in his eyes, countenance ashen and his entire body trembling, he grabbed me by my lapels and said, 'You'll get back to where you belong, if you know what's good for you!' It was half threat, half plea. Then bringing his hands in clenched fists up to his face to peer from behind invisible bars, he added, 'Otherwise, this is where you'll end up!' I had no idea what he was talking about. I should have.

Earlier that summer my father, a saintly and sensitive old man, then in his seventies, rang me early one Saturday morning in distress. He'd had a dark dream during the night and he pleaded with me to be careful. 'Son,' he said, 'there's an evil person involved somewhere in your life. There's something menacing about him. I can sense serious trouble ahead. Please be very careful.'

Oddly, although my father had never knowingly met Martin or his wife, still hasn't to my knowledge, I reminded him several years later of this conversation. I asked him if he could remember the man in his dream. He described Martin accurately – his distinctive physical appearance, his mannerisms and even the way in which he was manipulated by his wife.

And so it seemed that there was a wicked plan behind Martin's threats. Tom called one evening to tell me that a complaint had been lodged against me with the elders of the River of Life Fellowship. 'Complaint about what?' I asked. 'How could Martin have anything to complain about? He's my friend! He's been in my house group for years! Surely if he had something to complain about we would have sorted it out together. He has always trusted me and I have always been honest with him.'

But Tom wouldn't elaborate, and even the many private meetings Martin and I had had already, when it was obvious that something was building, did not prepare me for the mixed feelings of hurt, disappointment, confusion and fear. And then the pieces began to fall into place: my dad's dream; the tension in the atmosphere while we were on holiday; Martin's half threat, 'You'll get back to where you belong if you know what's good for you'; and the invisible prison bars. Perhaps naively I still chose to believe that, deep down, he wanted no part of it, that something or someone was manipulating him, driving him, and now the whole thing had taken on a life of its own. But I was misguided, so hard did I find it to believe that my 'good and faithful friend' could do such a thing.

As time passed it emerged that the complaint was that I had stolen money from Martin's business. He also had come to believe that the advice I had given him was more to my benefit than his. I can only speculate why he chose to do this. Perhaps he thought that God was using him to bring me down a peg or two. I was seen as a more successful businessman, a more confident and decisive person than he was, and that was interpreted as pride. But I had the feeling that while he was happy to trust me with the complicated financial matters relating to his business so long as I remained a brother, things were quite different once I'd left. Once out of the Fellowship I was no longer a brother. He had raised his concerns with the elders and they had done nothing to calm his fears, even though the allegations threatened to completely destroy my business.

It was obvious that the sorry saga could easily have been laid to rest by the leadership had the will been there, but clearly it wasn't. They had a vested interest in my disgrace and people can be good at believing what they want to believe. I think they saw this as a convenient and welcome opportunity for them to sit on their hands and observe my downfall. And why would they welcome that? Because they could point to me and say, 'That's what happens when you leave the covering.' Thus the leadership in an abusive church can reinforce their position of authority and control without damaging their squeaky-clean façade.

Even at this late stage, all would have been forgiven had I been prepared to recant and stay where the leaders felt I belonged. But my mind was made up, and I've often thought that the eagerness, if not glee, with which the elders presided over the developing proceedings demonstrated that they had more than a passing interest in the outcome. 'This,' they thought, 'is the story we need. This we will parade as Adam's hidden agenda.'

So serious were the allegations against me that it was decided to set up an ecclesiastical court. The theory was sound: as Christians we can sort out our disagreements without the need for recourse to the secular judicial system, and there is a biblical precedent for it.

> When you have something against another Christian, why do you file a lawsuit and ask a secular court to decide the matter, instead of taking it to other Christians to decide who is right? (1 Cor. 6:1).

I readily agreed to the idea, for although I knew I was totally innocent of the charges, the prospect of police action and possible judicial proceedings petrified me. I had never had any contact with the law enforcement agencies beyond an occasional parking ticket. Nor had I seen the inside of a police station, except on the few occasions when I was collecting money for charities.

David Robb, a respected Christian with considerable experience in the financial services business, agreed to stand as an independent arbitrator. All agreed that his findings would be binding; I would make full restitution or my accusers would withdraw all charges.

I shall never forget the pain I felt as I entered one of the rooms in the church building that doubled as a 'courtroom' that day, already half-filled with the some of the people whom I had addressed only months earlier, people with whom I had prayed and praised almost weekly for over ten years. But now the anger and suspicion in the atmosphere was obvious: nervous glances mingled with malevolent glares – already I had fallen victim to my pride, in their opinion. In my stubbornness, I had removed myself from under the covering and my fate was sealed.

The charges were read out. Although there was no mention of theft at this stage, it was alleged that I had forged Martin's signature on a legal document and I stood accused of fraud. At face value it looked bad, but viewed in context there was no case to answer. I had recommended that Martin should invest some of his company's profits in a company pension scheme, a widely accepted way of reducing tax liability. However, the tax laws stipulated that for tax relief to be granted, his cheque had to be lodged with the pensions company before the end of his financial year. The allegation was that in the frenzy of paperwork I had forgotten to get one of the forms signed, and as the deadline was looming, I signed Martin's name.

In the event, the verdict of the ecclesiastical court was that I was innocent. Yes, there was unprofessional conduct, but no fraud, no loss and no deceit. The anger and disappointment in that room was almost palpable. I felt hurt and betrayed; the innards of my business had been picked over and poked through in public, and even though I had been totally exonerated, it seemed that these folk, who had been my family for a quarter of my life, were determined to get me. And worse was to come.

> It is not an enemy who taunts me – I could bear that. It is not my foes who so arrogantly insult me – I could have hidden from them. Instead, it is you – my equal, my companion and close friend. What good fellowship we enjoyed as we walked together to the house of God (Ps. 55:12–14).

Regardless of the mutual commitment to accept the findings of the arbitrator, a complaint was lodged with the police Fraud Squad within days of the verdict, and an effective whispering campaign began. As many of my former clients as could be identified were approached and told that my business dealings were the subject of a police investigation. They were advised that it might be prudent to have the advice I had given them checked by a qualified third party. Some clients stayed with me, some switched to other financial advisors as rumours gathered pace, and a further two individuals, both from the River of Life Fellowship, also filed complaints with the police. Now while the elders did not make these calls, neither did they point to the findings of their own ecclesiastical court, nor did it seem was there any attempt to discourage the malice and lies that they must have known were crushing my family and me.

Over the next two years, friends and clients would call me. 'Adam, I've just had a visit from DS Johnston of the Fraud Squad. He's asking awkward questions. What's going on?' Most stuck loyally with me, but it became increasingly difficult for me to acquire new clients, and slowly my business went down the tubes. The Mercedes soon went. My entitlement to advance commissions paid to me by financial institutions ceased as former clients took their business elsewhere, and I found myself being pursued by them for the repayment of tens of thousands of pounds. The banks threatened foreclosure, the family home was at risk and the professional advice I sought told me to apply for self-administered bankruptcy.

Now, shame and indignity were added to isolation. Former friends vanished like summer snow. I had no job, no car, a sick wife, four children who had become used to the trappings of middle-class life, and my youngest son, an eight-year-old boy with learning difficulties, had been turned out of the little Christian school attached to the River of Life Fellowship. The nightmare had begun.

# CHAPTER 5

# THE NIGHTMARE BEGINS

We attached ourselves to the Belfast Christian Trust (BCT), the church that had grown out of the River of Life Fellowship in the early 1980s. But before long in BCT, a feeling grew that shepherding was still living and breathing under the shiny new veneer, and there was fresh discontent. So the elders of BCT did what Tom and his co-leaders had been unwilling to do – they courageously stood down en masse, publicly apologised, repented, asked for forgiveness and then presented themselves again for re-election. And most of them were re-elected, because while the members did not expect perfection, they appreciated honesty from their leaders.

BCT therefore, as a final product, appeared to incorporate all the advantages of the River of Life Fellowship, but without shepherding and enforced tithing pressing down on the people. There was good teaching, a lively youth department, and close and meaningful fellowship through cell groups. It was great. At last we had found a place that we could call our spiritual home, helped by the fact that we already knew many of the folk there. But then the ecclesiastical court met for the second time.

The first meeting of the court some months previously appeared to have been conclusive, but it was thought by the leaders in the Fellowship that a few details still needed to be ironed out, and so the court was reconvened in the early months of 1992 – significantly, in my new church. I didn't want to believe that the underlying purpose was to discredit me so I would not be accepted in my new spiritual home, but apparently, I needed to be purged. However, it was academic. As I had been reported to the Fraud Squad, whatever the ecclesiastical court decided would have made no difference to the police.

Ironically, I found a source of encouragement in a developing relationship with Daniel, who some years earlier had been in senior leadership in the River of Life Fellowship. I sought him out when it was becoming apparent that things were starting to get rough. We met in a little café near my home and I shall never forget the hammer-blow of his initial comment: 'When you leave, they kill you. They need to make an example of you, Adam, so that others who may be thinking of following you will have second thoughts.'

It was clear to the watchers in the Fellowship that I had found grace and acceptance in BCT, and there were early indications that a trickle was beginning to make its way from the River of Life Fellowship in the direction of BCT. It had to be stopped before it became the feared haemorrhage. But it could only be stopped if my shame was public and my destruction complete. David, one of the 'prophets' in the River of Life Fellowship made contact with Harry, the senior pastor of BCT, with a word that was supposedly from the Lord about me – 'Watch him.' That was hurtful when I found out, but I knew that my Father would never act in that way.

And so the ecclesiastical court was reconvened in BCT, with a specific request that a number of the leaders of BCT would be there to observe the proceedings. Tom strode into the building like a high court judge, with a bunch of official-looking files under his arm and an aide at his side. Harry asked, 'What's your role going to be here, Tom?' 'Everything!' was the predictable and arrogant reply. Harry melted into the background.

I was emotionally fragile. I was again being systematically humiliated and, combined with the prophetic word from David, I was made to feel like a pariah. I was not the sort of person any self-respecting pastor would want in his church. Thankfully, Harry was a generous man, with a humility that often comes with a legacy of suffering. He had learned from the early mistakes of BCT, and regardless of the implications of police interest in my business and David's 'prophetic word', he was prepared to take the risk and welcome us into the church. As a family we were quickly made to feel at home and were given space and time to get involved in a range of activities: home groups, music teams and all the rest. It seemed that our children, too, were instantly assimilated, and all the talk of dodgy business deals were either taken at face value with such comments as 'God is in the redemption business,' which indeed he is, or taken with a handful of salt. There was no apportioning of guilt, no condemnation and no accusing fingers. What a breath of fresh air! These precious people had an understanding of the immeasurable grace of God that I had never seen in a church before.

Predictably perhaps, nothing ever came of the second episode of the ecclesiastical court. It simply petered out, although it struck me as significant that David Robb was conspicuous by his absence. Presumably he wasn't to be trusted any more; he had backed the loser.

One of the elders of BCT happened to be a police inspector, who coincidentally had close connections with the Fraud Squad, and he was fully aware of what was going on behind the big steel gates at Castlereagh Police Station in East Belfast. Yet even this made no difference to the extent to which we as a family were accepted into genuine and warm fellowship. But there was still the hurdle of a police investigation for me to surmount.

In August 1993, I was preparing to go to my niece's wedding. It was one of those rare occasions when I was busy washing my car, when a gleaming, bright red car swept into my drive. I knew by the swagger of the big, silver-haired, immaculately dressed man who approached me that 'This was it!'

In a sense, it was a relief. For two years there had been phone calls from concerned friends and clients, and I knew that one day soon there would be the dreaded knock on the door. Now it was here and the uncertainty was gone.

It was like a scene from a movie: 'Are you Adam Harbinson?'

'Yes, I am.'

'I'm DS Johnston of the police Fraud Squad.'

'Yes, I know. I've been expecting you.' With a steely firmness and just a hint of compassion he agreed that, in the circumstances, our business could wait until tomorrow. 'But not a day longer.'

Next morning I rang my solicitor, a Christian friend whom I'd known for years, and he panicked. 'All we can hope for is damage limitation! This means a custodial sentence!' Damage limitation was all the poor man talked about for weeks as I reeled under the unthinkable prospect of a prison sentence.

Never one to tinker around the edges of a problem, I felt, despite being in a weakened emotional state, that the best form of defence was attack. I had to find a way to take the initiative. I was close to frantic and had to do something. Simply sitting around waiting, with no control over what might happen never was my strong point, so I went to the top. I located one of Ireland's top barristers, but an initial consultation with this individual cost almost a thousand pounds. I borrowed some money, made an appointment and arrived at his palatial office with my suitcase full of documents.

'How long have you been in business?' he asked after the initial pleasantries.

'Fifteen years.'

'How many clients do you have?'

'Around fifteen hundred.'

'How many complaints have been lodged against you?'

'Three.'

'When?'

'All in the last month.'

'And do they have anything in common?'

'Yes. All three are from people who belong to a Christian community I used to be part of.'

'Mr Harbinson,' he said as he closed his notebook. 'I wouldn't even bother opening that suitcase, which I presume contains your documents. I suggest you go home and forget all about this. You're the victim of a witch hunt.'

The best thousand pounds I ever spent!

But sadly it wasn't quite that simple. Neither DS Johnston nor my brothers and sisters in the Lord would easily forgo an opportunity to nail a rogue. And slowly, steadily he set about building his case. And it went on week after horrible week for over two years. Most of the allegations were spurious – laughable had the entire situation not been so tragic.

On one occasion the big sergeant held up a cheque for me to examine. 'Have you seen this cheque before?' It was from an insurance company, payable to Mr Martin Henshaw, and so I said yes. Martin had surrendered an insurance policy on my advice, and in those days the cheque from the insurance company would have been mailed to the broker, in this case me, to be passed on to the client.

'Mr Henshaw never saw this cheque, did he?' said the policeman. Then he turned the cheque around. 'Do you recognise the stamp on the reverse side of the cheque as that of your bank? You cashed this cheque and pocketed the money. Didn't you?' He was convinced that he had, finally, found something that looked like it might stick.

'Actually, no,' I said after a couple of minutes rummaging through my records. 'That's the stamp of Rachel's bank. Perhaps it was she who cashed the cheque and was happy for her husband to believe that I had stolen it,' and from that point, finally, his case began to fall apart. But I was shocked at the lengths to which former close friends would go to put me out of circulation and stunned that they could, so deliberately and without any rational purpose, ruin a friend, someone upon whom in happier times they had so heavily relied.

The other two members of the River of Life Fellowship who made charges had been particularly good friends too. Maureen's marriage had ended in tears a few years earlier and we took her in, prayed with her, wept with her, took her on holidays with us, shared our Christmas meal with her. She had become one of the family, and yet her allegation was so without substance that even the police didn't take it seriously. It was much the same with Philip. He and I had spent many hours together at various social and sporting events as well as the usual range of prayer meetings, home groups and the like, and while the allegations amounted to nothing and were quickly consigned to the bin, in a sense that wasn't the issue. I had accumulated over fifteen hundred clients and it would be silly to suggest that only three of them had any reason to complain. Financial Services can be intricate, misunderstandings can easily occur, and where there's money, there's often greed. So how could it be that the only three ever to complain were my brothers and sisters in the Lord?

To a point I could understand their hurt. I could see how they might have felt abused and betrayed by me. Perhaps they felt I had masqueraded as a friend and brother to win their trust so that I could gain access to their money. I've been through this a thousand times in my head, believe me. But however much I give them the benefit of the doubt, I don't think I'll ever fully understand why they did what they did. For example, Philip had agreed to increase his investment in an insurance policy by £15 a month six years previously. He paid the additional £15 every month for six years, and then complained that I had increased the contribution without his permission or knowledge. 'How could he do that?' I screamed in frustration at the big sergeant, and another contemptible allegation bit the dust.

I can only assume that they were all controlled by fear, which was driving them by means of some perverted herd instinct to protect their spiritual home, their pastor, their group identity. I was now an ex-member, an ex-brother and it was open season. It was the same spirit I saw in Martin's eyes that night, in spite of his love for me. And yes, without being melodramatic, I do believe that dark and evil powers were at work. Paul the apostle wrote:

> For we are not fighting against people made of flesh and blood [not Martin and Rachel, Philip and Maureen, not even Tom] ,'but against the evil rulers and authorities of the unseen world, against those mighty powers of

darkness who rule this world, and against wicked spirits in the heavenly realms (Eph. 6:12).

My understanding of that Scripture enabled me to see past my accusers to the dark forces ranged behind them, but the challenge for me was to recognise that while they had chosen to do a great evil, they too were victims. They were being manipulated to do what would never have occurred to them to do in the normal course of events. But whether victims or willing perpetrators, to gloss over what they had done would be to dilute the power of grace and forgiveness. Yes I can and must forgive them, but the reality is, you can't forgive someone without first acknowledging that there's something to forgive. They had conducted themselves in a most wicked way, determined to inflict maximum damage without rigorously examining what it was they were accusing me of, and without considering the impact their behaviour would have on a family.

It's twelve years since those times, but the memory of that police investigation, the hum of the tape recorder in Interview Room 101, the bankruptcy, the cold shoulders from one-time friends, the sense of failure, the humiliation, the utter desolation and loneliness and vulnerability of it all, still seizes my gut with an icy terror. There's something about your home that makes you feel safe. It's a haven: you can close the door and keep predators and dangers at bay, but as a suspect under police investigation even that basic security was gone. There were a couple of occasions when the big sergeant or one of his emissaries arrived on my doorstep late on a Sunday evening – 'Just to make sure you'll turn up in the morning.' The dread that I longed to shield my family from, by keeping it restricted to police station, invaded even the sanctuary of my home.

Each week, I'd be in that interview room deep in the forbidding police station for hours at a time: being ground down, being made to feel guilty and dirty, wanting it all to go away at any price. Once or twice I was so scared that I called on the telephone and asked to be excused 'just this once'. Instead of meeting compassion, I was threatened with arrest: 'The blue lights will be flashing at your front door before you put the receiver down.'

One Sunday evening, I could not face the prospect of another Monday morning's interrogation session and, late in the evening, I called our family GP. Richard was a Christian too, a lifelong friend who would walk through some more of life's hard roads with us in the future. 'I just can't do it, Richard,' I pleaded. 'Can you call him in the morning; tell him I'm medically unfit; tell him anything?' But Richard was a police surgeon and knew the form. Rather than being excused, I got a dose of pethidine in my rear-end that put me out of action for 48 hours. But fraud squads don't go away that easily, and Wednesday morning I was back in room 101, with the tape recorder running. To this day if I'm watching a movie in which there's a scene in a police interview room, it's the sight and sound of the tape recorder running that turns my blood cold.

Daphne had contracted breast cancer in 1983, just weeks after Jonny, our fourth child, was born. She'd had radical surgery: a breast removed, a couple of courses of radiotherapy followed by chemtherapy and a course of pills that she would take for the rest of her life. Physically and emotionally she had been weakened by recurring bouts of lupus and sarcoidosis as well as the toxicity of chemotherapy, and then there was the added strain of dealing with a new baby with a number of disabilities. Now she was heading for a breakdown. The only thing that kept us going in those dark and awful days was the prospect that one day it would all be over. One day we would be able to make some sense of it all.

Sometimes I would call my father. He would bring together a group of his saintly old friends and they would pray for me during the hours I was incarcerated. I could often feel the warm arms of my Father enfolding me in that cold, intimidating place, and at times I wished I could wake up from the fearful nightmare. But I was discovering something else not much talked about – character building. In my daily devouring of the Bible, I found a promise to God's people spoken through Isaiah: 'When you go through deep waters and great trouble, I will be with you. When you go through rivers of difficulty, you will not drown! When you walk through the fire of oppression, you will not be burned up; the flames will not consume you' (Is. 43:2). Three times there Isaiah said 'when'; not once did he say 'if'.

It was bizarre. Alan (I had begun to develop a relationship of sorts with DS Johnston) had gone to get me a coffee and a chocolate biscuit – 'Bring me a Breakaway,' I would joke. I was standing with my back to a gurgling radiator in an effort to get a modicum of heat into my shivering bones, and my mind turned to my old dad. I knew he'd be praying for me at that very moment, and a feeling of overwhelming love swept over me. But it wasn't just an appreciation of my dad's love for me; I was beginning to learn something of the Father's love. Why else would he choose to be with me in the floods and in the intense heat of the fires if he didn't love me greatly?

I've already mentioned Jesus' story of the Prodigal Son in another context, but now for the first time I could see, only dimly at first, that the central character in the story isn't the boy at all, it's the story of a prodigal father.

It's about the absurd grace and reckless love of the father. That's what the word 'prodigal' means – reckless and extravagant. And the penny began to drop.

'I'm walking through some pretty hot fires here, and I could do with an extinguisher. But I'm not getting scorched, and I'm not alone. There are ferocious waves crashing all around me, but they are not sweeping over my head.' What was happening? God, who had not ordained these painful times, was using them to build character, to prepare me for what might lie ahead. Just as Joseph's time in prison honed the qualities he needed for his role as Prime Minister of Egypt. Just as Moses' forty years tending his uncle's flocks in the desert prepared him for the otherwise impossible task of shepherding God's flock for another forty years. God was with Joseph in prison, he was with Moses in the desert, and he was with me in Castlereagh Police Station in East Belfast.

And as I stood with my back to the radiator, in the bowels of a police station, with all these thoughts running through my head, it dawned on me: my spirit was free. With God I was invincible. And I wondered if there would ever come a day when I could look back over the years and say, as Joseph said to his brothers who had sold him into slavery, 'God turned into good what you meant for evil' (Gen. 50:20).

Another morning, as I prayed for the nightmare to go away, the story of the caterpillar, the cocoon and the dead butterfly came into my mind. A little boy and his granddad walked through the fields together enjoying the late spring sunshine. The boy found a caterpillar that had spun a cocoon around itself where it would be safe until it metamorphosed into a butterfly. They looked on at one of nature's wonders as the cocoon cracked and the butterfly struggled to shake off the shell that would keep it earthbound. The boy thought he would help, and the old man looked on as gently the child cracked open the cocoon and the butterfly fell to the ground, unable to flap its wings. It was only in the struggle to break free from the chains of its past that it would gain the strength needed to do what it was created for – to fly.

And all the time the whispering campaign continued. It was hurtful to watch my family go through all that suffering, for at times I felt responsible. And it was doubly painful to realise that my brothers and sisters, some of whom could have easily have shouted 'Enough!' seemed truly to believe that I was getting my come-uppance. But those who had made the charges and could easily have withdrawn them, didn't, for there was no place for mercy in their religious psyche. And it wasn't just the lies that were being spread, it was the readiness of many to embrace them, people from whom I would have expected a little support. It was the fact that some of those with whom I sincerely believed I'd had a close relationship, who knew that my family was falling apart, did nothing, showed no interest, didn't call, offered no help. How precious a letter, a knock on the door or a telephone call would have been. Even five or six years later when my wife died, there was still no response from this community of God's people, no sign of life, nothing. We had simply slid off the radar. We had ceased to exist.

The chap who had been my shepherd was now involved in mission work. On a trip back to Ireland from Africa where he was building a nationwide medical service, he dropped in to see us. He had heard that Daphne had cancer, and as we talked about the events of the preceding couple of years, he said, 'But I know these people, Adam. They really mean you no harm.'

'They mean me no harm! What planet are you on?' I roared. 'They're trying to put me in jail! They've made no attempt to prevent the destruction of my business and now you'd think they were doing their level best to deprive my family of fellowship in BCT!' But he couldn't see it. Perhaps he didn't want to see it; this was the due process of the law, nothing more.

Our attendance at BCT became less regular. There was one Sunday morning when, facing the prospect of another visit to the police station next day, I sought the sanctuary of prayer. My heart was breaking; my family looked like it was beginning to fall apart. My wife was questioning my judgement and possibly my innocence too, by this stage. So at the end of the service I made my way to the prayer room, with Daphne trotting reluctantly behind, in search of comfort or a scrap of encouragement. Harry happened to be there and he prayed for me, and as I sat, trembling, perhaps having my nineteenth nervous breakdown, I happened to open my eyes and caught sight of Harry, sitting beside me with his big gentle hand on my back. He was looking at his watch.

'Tell you what,' says he, 'let's leave this for a while. We'll pray together again.' The odd thing was that whilst it was obvious that I was coming between him and his Sunday lunch, I had a sense that somehow, amid the trauma and confusion, the rejection, the pain, the guilt and the mess of it all, the path out of it and its timing would be of God's choosing. It would all make sense in the end. I think that's what faith is.

I stopped going to church. It was becoming embarrassing. The last time I attended BCT was on a Sunday evening. We sang the beautiful Brian Doerksen song 'Faithful One', and by the time we got to the end of the first verse, I was reduced to a blubbering heap on the floor. My wife was embarrassed now too. Janet, the wife of one of the elders made her way from her seat on the front row to where I was on the back row. How she knew

I was there, I'd no idea, I was sure I was crying quietly. She placed her hand on my brow and simply said, 'Our God is the God of the second chance and the third chance ...' Under the power of that moment I broke, again, and the rest of her words were drowned out by my convulsive sobbing. That's why it was embarrassing to go to church. I wanted to sing, I loved to sing, but every time I opened my mouth, all I could do was weep.

This was my wilderness experience. I no longer felt comfortable in church. I felt like the patient who turned up in the doctor's surgery twice a week, every week. But a strange change was taking place. I was developing an insatiable hunger for God's company and for the Bible, and for the first time in my life I was gaining the ability – and the courage – to think independently of the religious establishment in which I had been brought up and to which I had felt attached for over a decade.

At this point I had no job, although I was doing some post-grad work on criminology at university as well as selling advertising in an effort to make ends meet. I had time to read for hours each day, and often well into the night. But at first, the more I read the more depressed I became, and the reason was that I was seeing everything through the lens of the River of Life Fellowship. I would read Deuteronomy 28:15–18:

> If you refuse to listen to the LORD your God and do not obey all the commands and laws I am giving you today, all these curses will come and overwhelm you: You will be cursed in your towns and in the country. You will be cursed with baskets empty of fruit and with kneading bowls empty of bread ...

Now that is one scary chapter to read. It made me feel that God was taking over from where the elders of the River of Life Fellowship had left off. Their behaviour was vindicated. I was finished, without hope, out from under the covering, rejected by God and heading for damnation. But I had been brought up to believe that God is good and that Jesus paid the penalty for my wrongdoing, and so I persevered, hoping, mostly against hope, that soon a light would dawn, soon he would rescue me. And he did, for I found Psalm 103:10 – 'He has not punished us for all our sins, nor does he deal with us as we deserve. For his unfailing love toward those who fear him is as great as the height of the heavens above the earth.'

I so much needed to hear that. And I read on with gathering excitement, 'He has removed our rebellious acts as far away from us as the east is from the west.' I wish I could put into words the joy and the freedom those words spoke to my heavy, hungry heart. And then it got better, for I came across 2 Corinthians 5:21, 'For God made Christ, who never sinned, to be the offering for our sin, so that we could be made right with God through Christ.' That did two things for me. Firstly it squared the circle of Deuteronomy 28 – all those horrible curses in store for those who do not keep the letter of God's law were borne by Jesus. And all the blessings that were due to him as a result of his spotless life, they all come to us. But, more fundamentally, I began to see that my mind needed to be 'mucked out' by a process of unlearning decades of dodgy doctrines, and an enthralling journey that still captivates me had begun.

> I was an angry, wounded person emerging from a toxic church, and I've been in recovery ever since. (Philip Yancey)[6]

From that moment on, I began to read the Bible as if I had never read it before. Everything was fresh and new. It was like reading tomorrow morning's newspaper: no paradigms; no little boxes into which everything fitted neatly; no tidy, sterile answers to a prayer so deep it cannot be spoken.

The last time I attended the police station was an ordeal that I found so terrifying I could easily have cracked and admitted to a crime that I did not commit. As I entered Interview Room 101 there was a stack of files on the desk. They were piled so high that it looked like they might topple at any moment, and beside them on the same desk lay a single, thin brown-coloured folder.

'It's time to end this charade, Adam,' said Alan. 'But it's down to you whether we do it the hard way or the easy way.' And he gave me the option, 'Make a statement now, admit your guilt and you'll be home in time for lunch. There's paper and a pen in there,' he said pointing to the thin brown folder. 'The alternative is for us to go through each file in that pile, one at a time. You'll be here every day for the next six months – your choice!'

I eyed the skyscraper pile of accusations as it threatened to fall over and finally crush me. How good it would be to be home for lunch: no more veiled threats, no more panic attacks, no more sweat-soaked dreams in the night, no more DS Johnston. A court case, yes, but at least I wouldn't be alone. I would have an advocate, and I'd have my family around me. I took the piece of paper out from the folder and held it in my hand. This was my easy way out. This would make it all go away. 'What do you want me to write?' I asked naively.

'Just tell the truth.'

So I asked him for a Breakaway biscuit, a coffee, and for fifteen minutes to think. He obliged, and when he returned in fifteen minutes the biscuit was still in its wrapper and the coffee was cold, but I had made my statement. I told him my story. I told him it was all a wicked ploy by people who were driven by fear, whose lives were dedicated to meaningless little power games, who talked much about love but who knew only a love that seeks in others the fulfilment of its own desires.

'I'm innocent, Alan, and whatever it takes, and however long it takes, we'll go through that scary pile – one page at a time if necessary!' I'm so glad my old dad was praying at that very moment for God to empower me to make the right decision.

Strangely, I was indeed home for lunch. For reasons that I can only speculate about, not a single one of that stack of files was opened. Perhaps it was because someone was praying, perhaps there was a rational explanation, I still don't know, but I didn't care, for the ordeal was finally over. And I managed a joke. It even made Alan laugh. As he had done at the end of each interview for over two years, he slid a piece of paper across the desk, asking me to sign it to confirm that I hadn't been badly treated. With a sly little grin, I slid it back and said, 'Do you want me to write my signature here, Alan, or yours?'

I arrived home that day with a rare spring in my step. It was a Friday, and for the first time in over two years we could look forward to a family weekend that was not pervaded at every level by the dread of another Monday morning. I was in my mid-forties, with almost nothing to show for half a lifetime's work. The middle-class trappings had gone, but we were experiencing true prosperity, for we took time for walks in the woods, for skimming stones at the beach and for family meals. And occasionally in the evenings we would scrape together a few pounds to rent a video, buy some pizzas and laugh again. We owned our home but that was about all we had, and yet years later when my daughter had come home from university for a couple of days and we talked again about that difficult time, she said, 'That was when I got my daddy back.'

The worst of my nightmare was over, although the sword of Damocles still hung by a single horsehair over my head, for Alan assured me that the Director of Public Prosecutions would follow his recommendations and prosecute. It took perhaps another year before I could fully rest in the belief that the threat of imprisonment was history. But in spite of this, I was experiencing a degree of freedom that I had never thought possible. Not only were the bonds of control and manipulation that lay at the heart of the shepherding movement gone but, most of all, I was free from the debilitating fear that I might not measure up to the standard God required. I was free from the crushing burden of always having to try harder, pray more, read the Bible more and go to more meetings in a relentless and needless striving to please a God who is already delighted with me.

Yet I knew I would never be totally free until all traces of fear had gone. I believed that when the time was right, God would have me stride with poise and godly confidence into the very seat of the community that had contributed to my heartbreak and ruin and that of many others. And so at Christmas time, twelve years after I left, I returned with my new family. Daphne had long since lost her battle with cancer, Simon was working as a GP in Scotland, Sarah was teaching in Rwanda, Timothy was studying English at Glasgow University and Jonny was in the process of moving into his own little flat near my new home where we could keep an eye on him. I was now married to Pauline, and I had acquired another three great children: Stephanie (17),

Matthew (15) and Peter (10). The fact that I had begun a completely new chapter in my life made it all the more urgent for me to lay my final ghost of the past to rest.

I was nervous at first as we walked through doors that I thought I would never darken again, but we were well accepted and most people seemed not just surprised but genuinely pleased to see us. Tom avoided eye contact for a while, but in the end he too offered a warm embrace. It was gracious of him. Many painful memories were stirred and it took a further four or five visits before I could look each member there straight in the face and honestly feel, 'This place, these people no longer have a hold over me. Some of them may have intended to harm me, but God intended it all for good'.

Thus I made my statement of trust in the faithfulness of the Good Shepherd who had replaced the savage shepherds in my life. I was walking under the banner of the One who knew the limit of my endurance and would not have me pushed beyond it, who had stood with me as flames licked around me and as great waves crashed about me. At last I knew I was free!

# CHAPTER 6

# THE STRUGGLE WITH FORGIVENESS

Daniel had told me, 'When you leave, they kill you!' He also said that such is the nature and extent of the damage caused by spiritual abuse, it could take several years to recover fully, if ever. How right he was. Even as I write, after almost fifteen years, I remain keenly aware of a certain rawness in some deep recesses of my life that still causes me to overreact to anything that smells of manipulation or control.

I found it difficult to forgive those whom I had trusted so completely. I felt I had been comprehensively violated. I was angry and yet I felt stupid for walking into such a situation with my eyes wide open, and remaining there for over a decade! For years after I left, I was sure I could never darken the door of that place again, and there were times when I felt my children were being disloyal to me when they attended a concert or a party in the building. On one occasion, when I met Tom at a family funeral and he offered a handshake, I surprised myself at the extent of my rudeness: I coldly looked him straight in the eye and quite deliberately turned my back and walked way.

I found many words to excuse my feelings and behaviour, but I knew the truth – it was deep-seated unforgiveness. I was frustrated because I expected to be able to deal with it immediately. Ordinarily I'm not one to carry grudges. However, I now see that forgiveness is not only part of the healing process, it is itself a process. It can take time and must be allowed time, for if rushed, the result can be that the issues are suppressed and buried. But they're buried alive, they can burst back onto the scene at an inappropriate time to surprise and cause further damage.

I wanted my forgiveness of those guys to be instant, because my evangelical upbringing had taught me to keep 'a short account with God'. I need God's forgiveness, but I had always been taught that God's forgiveness is conditional. My impatience and frustration with myself was growing by the day because of my understanding of a couple of little verses tacked onto the end of what we now call the Lord's Prayer:

> If you forgive those who sin against you, your heavenly Father will forgive you. But if you refuse to forgive others, your Father will not forgive your sins (Mt. 6:14,15).

Some commentators suggest that these two verses are Matthew's equivalent of Mark 11:25 where Jesus makes a very similar statement:

> But when you are praying, first forgive anyone you are holding a grudge against, so that your Father in heaven will forgive your sins, too.

I was finding it difficult to forgive those who had done so much damage to my business, my family and my health, although I knew that God was nudging me gently along the way. I came face to face with Ben, one of the elders who had been most active in nailing my hide to the wall. Every day for a couple of weeks when his wife was confined to bed and as I was doing the school-run, I met him on the road as he was picking his boy up from school. Sometimes our eyes would meet in one of those hesitant 'do-I-acknowledge-or-do-I-not-acknowledge?' moments. Sometimes I would nod or faintly smile through gritted teeth, at other times I would pretend I didn't see him, and yes, there were times when I was deliberately rude. However, there was one occasion when I had just written an article about forgiveness – wearing my newspaper columnist hat – and I felt pricked in my conscience.

Here was I, pontificating about the peace and sense of release that comes when you forgive someone who has wronged you. 'Forgiveness is a decision, not a feeling,' I spouted. 'If you refuse to forgive, or feel that you cannot, it can screw you up inside while the object of your bitterness may be sailing through life blissfully unaware of your internal anguish.' That was the gist of my column that week. And then I saw Ben, so when I got home I rang him.

'Ben,' said I, 'there are times when I really struggle with what happened with Martin and Rachel, and in particular your role in the incident. But I'd like to think that now we can draw a line under it and put things right between us. It's not right for brothers to meet and be unable to look each other in the eye. Can we meet for a coffee and a yarn?'

And his reaction surprised me. 'No, Adam. There's absolutely no chance of any reconciliation between you and me.' Click! However, the problem was no longer mine, it was his, although I found it hard to understand how and why an individual who was a church leader and a shepherd could be so brutal. But I learned something else from that brief encounter. Much of our pain, our disappointment and our feelings of rejection arise from unrealistic expectations. Yes, Ben was an elder in his local church, but I have no right to expect more of him than of others, simply because of his perceived standing. And while it's true that James in his New Testament letter said, 'For we who teach will be judged by God with greater strictness' (Jas. 3:1) – that's between him and God.

This has been reinforced a number of times for me in recent years. It's often the case that those who judge others most harshly are those who have most deceit in their lives. Perhaps it's something to do with the specks of sawdust, planks of wood and hypocrites that Jesus spoke about in the Sermon on the Mount (Mt. 7:3–5). I can think of another Christian leader who was also involved in the witch hunt against me. It emerged years later that, even as he was enthusiastically inflicting maximum damage on one of his brothers, he was engaged in a long-standing affair that eventually resulted in a damaged marriage, a weakened church and hurting children. We will continue to be disappointed and hurt as long as we attribute status to any individual because of their position in the church. And I sometimes wonder why it is that we so easily and so often miss what Jesus had to say about the Pharisees of his day:

> The religion scholars and Pharisees are competent teachers in God's law. You won't go wrong in following their teachings on Moses. But be careful about following *them*. They talk a good line, but they don't live it. They don't take it into their hearts and live it out in their behaviour. It's all spit-and-polish veneer.
>
> Instead of giving you God's law as food and drink by which you can banquet on God, they package it in bundles of rules, loading you down like pack animals. They

seem to take pleasure in watching you stagger under these loads, and wouldn't think of lifting a finger to help. Their lives are perpetual fashion shows, embroidered prayer shawls one day and flowery prayers the next. They love to sit at the head table at church dinners, basking in the most prominent positions, preening in the radiance of public flattery, receiving honorary degrees, and getting called "Doctor" and "Reverend."

Don't let people do that to *you*, put you on a pedestal like that. You all have a single Teacher, and you are all classmates. Don't set people up as experts over your life, letting them tell you what to do. Save that authority for God; let *him* tell you what to do. . . (Mt. 23:2–8 The Message).

Jesus made it clear in those few sentences how we should relate to those in leadership in the church. Don't be a sheep if that means placing anyone on a pedestal in your life, and don't be a shepherd if that requires you to lord it over people: not ever.

However, my main concern was that while I was a child of God – I acknowledged Jesus as my Saviour, I'd said the 'sinner's prayer' and all the rest – my fundamentalist background had taught me that if, in a moment of unforgiveness, I were to be hit by a bus, I could find myself standing before the Judgement Seat of Christ with some very awkward questions to answer.

One day, as I was wrestling with these things, an old friend of my dad's rang my doorbell. Andrew was a Bible teacher. He'd been Principal of a Bible college somewhere in Africa, responsible for over twenty churches there, and he had taken to visiting me regularly. I was sure he could help.

'Andrew,' I gushed after a few initial niceties, 'do you believe in the finished work of Christ? Do you believe that by his life, death and resurrection our salvation is

totally procured or is there something we need to add?'
He assured me that he believed in the total sufficiency of
Calvary – there was nothing to add.

'But,' I stammered, 'please explain for me Matthew
6:14,15: ". . . if you refuse to forgive others, your Father
will not forgive your sins."' I wasn't trying to trick him,
I honestly wasn't. I was engaged in a titanic spiritual
and intellectual struggle and at times felt that I was
going under because, on the face of it, it seemed to me
that the cross of Christ is only complete when my forgiveness is added. But Andrew looked at his watch and
exclaimed, 'Good gracious, is that the time? Norma will
have my lunch ready, I must be off.' That's fourteen
years ago, and I haven't seen or heard from him since.

Why couldn't he have had the humility to say, 'I don't
know either' – for it was obvious that he didn't – 'but I
agree it looks like a problem text. Let's work together
with it to see if we can unravel it in a way that glorifies
Jesus rather than minimises his sacrifice.' But instead, it
seems that when there's something in Scripture that
we've always been taught – our denominational mind-
sets – rather than grappling with it and challenging our
paradigms, rather than looking to the Spirit of Truth to
unpack mysteries that might call upon us to reshape our
thinking, we skirt around it. Worse still, we attempt to
shoehorn our doctrines into Scripture, or vice versa, and
we miss the exciting enlightenment of God's word.

For me this was crucial – so crucial that I could not let
it go. If, as it appeared to me, our forgiveness and as a
consequence our eternal well-being depend on us living
in total and constant forgiveness toward others, then we
are all on exceedingly shaky ground. And I still find
it difficult to understand why I have never heard it
expounded, not once in half a century of church
attendance. I couldn't find anyone who had tackled the

issue in print either. For example in D. L. Moody's *Notes from My Bible*, the extent of his observation is, 'Christ said "Forgive to be forgiven". Paul said, "Forgive because forgiven".' And that's it, apart from pointing his readers to Ephesians 4:32: 'Be kind to each other, tenderhearted, forgiving one other, just as God through Christ has forgiven you.'

Now admittedly, a little light is thrown on the subject there because Paul uses the past tense: 'God through Christ *has* forgiven you.' But had something happened between Jesus' and Paul's statements to move the goal-posts, or is there another explanation? Firstly, as I saw it, Paul refers to the gospel as 'My gospel' (Rom. 2:16, 2 Tim. 2:8). Did he mean his gospel was different from Jesus' gospel? Are there two distinct and competing gospels? And given that an event of cosmic proportions did take place between those two utterances, the crucifixion of Jesus, did that cosmic event render Jesus' statement obsolete? Had things already moved on?

The writer to the Hebrews makes a number of significant statements on the subject. In chapter 8 he says, 'If the first covenant had been faultless, there would have been no need for a second covenant to replace it.' And then there follows a quote from Jeremiah 31 offering a little more clarification: 'The day will come, says the Lord, when I will make a new covenant with the people of Israel and Judah . . . I will forgive their wrongdoings, and I will never again remember their sins.' And the writer concludes with the summary: 'When God speaks of a 'new' covenant, it means he has made the first one obsolete.'

Again in the letter to the Hebrews it is made clear that a will comes into force only when the person who made the will has died (Heb. 9:16,17) – we all know that. So it would appear that under Paul's teaching, that will, the

New Covenant or New Testament, had come into force now that Jesus had died. Could it be that under the terms of that new arrangement we have been forgiven unconditionally, regardless of whether or not we forgive those who harm us? And is this why Paul was able to say, 'forgiving one another, just as God through Christ has forgiven you' (Eph. 4:32)?

Perhaps, but there are difficulties with this analysis, in that it could be taken to imply a degree of conflict between Jesus' gospel and Paul's gospel, or that one is a development of the other. The alternative is to consider the fact that both Jesus' statements in Matthew 6:14,15 and Mark 11:25 were made in the context of prayer, something I had always overlooked. Therefore, it would appear that God's reluctance to forgive those who do not forgive is not in the context of the Christian's salvation. The context is in the effectiveness of prayer.

I believe that Matthew is following Mark here and saying that the prayers of the church will never be mountain-moving while unforgiveness (or what Yancey calls ungrace) rules in the church. Disunity and strife between Christian brothers and sisters in a church causes their communal praying to be ineffective. Father won't forgive those who don't forgive, the channel is blocked between the family and the Father while there is bitterness in the family. According to commentator Tom Long,[7] forgiveness is so central to the Christian life that it is like breathing: inhale – receive God's forgiveness; exhale – dispense God's forgiveness.

Viewed against the backdrop of the broad sweep of Scripture, there is no alternative but to lean towards the latter analysis, that Matthew 6:14,15 and Mark 11:25 were speaking in the context of prayer, although perhaps a fuller understanding draws a little from both analyses. However, there are some indisputable truths beyond doubt or debate that we should focus on, the starting point being Ephesians 2:8: 'God saved you by his special favour when you believed. And you can't take credit for this; it is a gift from God. Salvation is not a reward for the good things we have done, so none of us can boast about it.'

Salvation is all of grace; there is nothing for us to add. Grace is God's undeserved favour, defined as 'the merciful kindness by which God, exerting his holy influence upon souls, turns them to Christ, keeps, strengthens and increases them in Christian faith.'[8] God takes the initiative, and if he takes the initiative, he will not in the next moment place obstacles and impossible conditions in the path of forgiveness and reconciliation.

In Paul's letter to the Colossians (3:13) he encourages them and us to 'make allowance for each other's faults and forgive the person who offends you. Remember, the Lord forgave you, so you must forgive others.' Again, in his letter to the Ephesians (4:32) he exhorts: 'Be kind to each other, tenderhearted, forgiving one another, just as God through Christ has forgiven you'. The readiness with which Jesus offers forgiveness – one could say it's his 'default position' – can be seen in Mark 2:5: 'Seeing their faith, Jesus said to the paralysed man, "My son, your sins are forgiven".' There's no record of the crippled man asking for forgiveness, far less being required to meet tough conditions.

For me, the conclusion is well summed up by L. Gregory Jones, 'God forgives us before we repent. Our repentance is an outworking of that forgiveness.'[9]

# CHAPTER 7

# THE TOOLS OF THE ABUSER'S TRADE

Many people who have had no experience of abusive churches can find it hard to understand why members don't simply leave. It's not that easy! What I was up against, what all church members are up against in these situations, was deception. And deception is at its most effective when it promotes a belief that is almost true. Sorting out the good from the bad – in an atmosphere where such analysis was frowned on – was extremely difficult.

I did, however, maintain a certain measure of mental independence – and it didn't add to my popularity, particularly when I was questioning the biblical basis of their teaching. My view always was that if the teacher was uncomfortable with my reluctance to believe and follow them without question, that was their problem, and if things boiled over, which occasionally they did, I simply reminded them of the example of the 'noble Bereans' and the immediate situation was usually defused in a fairly good spirit – my compass bearing being that it's the teacher's responsibility to teach, but it is the responsibility of those who listen to test the speaker:

Dear friends, do not believe everyone who claims to speak by the Spirit. You must test them to see if the spirit they have comes from God. For there are many false prophets in the world (1 Jn 4:1,2).

It was said of the Bereans that '. . . they listened eagerly to Paul's message. They searched the Scriptures day after day to see if Paul and Silas were teaching the truth' (Acts 17:11). Now bearing in mind who this Paul was – the one whom God entrusted to bring us the gospel, (Gal. 1:12) the man who bequeathed us more than half the New Testament – it would have been quite remarkable by our standards for these ordinary folk to be checking up on him. And yet Luke described the Bereans as being noble for going to the trouble of scrutinising the Great Apostle (Acts 17:11 NIV)!

Truthfully, how often do you or I rush home from church on a Sunday morning and examine the Scriptures to see if what the preacher said was true? And here's a searching question with a telling answer: how do you think your minister/pastor would feel if he thought you were following the example of the noble Bereans?

The leaders of the River of Life Fellowship were afraid that if we, the sheep, were to engage in independent study of the Bible and to have an independent relationship with God, we might see and understand something that would empower us, indeed provoke us, to challenge their position of absolute power.

> A pastor would violate his ecclesiastical power to control, manipulate and shame his congregation in order to secure his position and lust for power. (Marc Dupont)[10]

The sheep were never discouraged from reading the Bible, but there were handouts with extensive footnotes, and endless meetings, instructing us how texts should be interpreted. And home groups were carefully monitored too, usually being encouraged to study a book systematically, approved by the leaders of course. Flying through the Bible solo was frowned upon.

However, running parallel to their insistence that shepherds had the sole right to interpret Scripture for the sheep, was an almost pathological reliance on the theology embedded in some of the old hymns, particularly those of Charles Wesley, William Cowper, John Newton and Gerhard Tersteegen. There was one occasion when I dared to question the words of a fine old hymn. It seemed to me that the writer might have got it wrong.

'The words are truly beautiful,' I suggested, 'but could it be that they are theologically flawed?' The room went deathly still; what heretic had dared to question the integrity of a revered man of God? But I had a sincere difficulty with the words in the third verse of the hymn – the suggestion that my human failings would drive the Holy Spirit away from me when I needed him most:

> Return, O holy Dove, return,
> Sweet messenger of rest;
> I hate the sins that made thee mourn,
> And drove thee from my breast.[11]

'Surely,' I appealed, 'it cannot be that when I stray from the path and need his loving arms around me, he leaves me until I get myself sorted out. And if this is so, is it only when I'm squeaky-clean again that he will return? Did he not promise 'I will never fail you. I will never forsake you' (Heb 13:5)?

It seemed that even the liberating power and simplicity of God's word were diluted by the fact that it was a mere sheep who was using it as a yardstick to measure the truth. My pleas for good sense were ignored. The fact is that we are all human, but the very suggestion that even saintly hymn writers can get it wrong was heresy to the leaders of the Fellowship. The issue raised in the hymn, which is profound in the extreme for it goes to the very core of the Christian faith, was to my knowledge never discussed or scrutinised, and it continues to this day to be sung unthinkingly by many.

On numerous occasions as we lustily sang the wonderful words of *Thou Hidden Source of Calm Repose, And Can It Be* or *Rejoice, the Lord is King*, the experience was spoiled for me by the popular claim in the Fellowship that these hymns could be inspired by the Holy Spirit, in the same way as the Bible was – a sure recipe for dodgy doctrines. But my suspicion was and is, that it was part of the process of censoring what we were to believe by promoting and building on the thoughts and theology of individuals who bore the official stamp of approval. Or perhaps it was a result of their system of thought that grew out of the obsession with authority in the shepherding movement, which in turn grew out of their belief that God was like them: judgmental, quick to condemn, slow to forgive and reluctant to forget.

We were taught that when the Holy Spirit descended on Jesus at his baptism, he was likened to a dove, but this analogy was taken to an absurd extreme. We were reminded that a dove is a timid bird. If you make a sudden move, or clap your hands, the bird will fly away, only to return, if at all, when things have quietened down again. The words, 'I hate the sins that made thee mourn and drove thee from my breast', effectively instilled in us a fear that our humanness would alienate us from the Holy Spirit because he resembles a faint-hearted dove who needs to be tiptoed around, not to say patronised. This discourages us from being real with God.

Thankfully however, the truth is quite the contrary. There have been many times in my life when I have been saddened, angered, hurt or disappointed, and I've always found God to be robust enough to absorb my outbursts. I have stood at the side of an open grave and hurled unrepeatable abuse in his face, and still his loving arms enfolded me. That's how deeply secure we can be in our relationship with him, although I don't recommend it as a regular practice. He will never manipulate us or control our behaviour by threatening to go off in a huff if we are 'naughty children'. But sadly, it's always easier to persist in holding to a dubious doctrine that is deeply embedded in the culture and ideology of a community, than it is to adopt or even consider a truth that challenges it.

It is perhaps no coincidence that such groups give greater priority to praise and worship – singing, drama, dance or whatever – than the more traditional churches do. And while this is as it should be, there is a subtlety of which we need to be aware. It is of course true that we are encouraged to 'Give honour to the Lord for the glory of his name. Worship the Lord in the splendour of his holiness' (Ps. 29:2), and corporate worship is a vital and legitimate part of the Christian life. However, relying on an obscure verse taken from the King James Version (KJV) – the only occasion on which I ever remember the KJV being relied upon in the River of Life Fellowship – we were taught that God lived in our praises; 'O thou that inhabitest the praises of Israel' (Ps. 22:3). The *New Living Translation* renders that Scripture, 'The praises of Israel surround your throne,' and the *New International Version*, the version of the Bible that we normally used, translates the same verse 'You are the praise of Israel'.

But neither of those versions was in line with the River of Life Fellowship's theology.

The implication was that only if our worship was to the required standard would God deign to come down from heaven and grace us with his presence. The down side, of course, was that if our worship was not up to scratch, then God would stay put with his back toward us – cold, displeased and distant in his far-off holy heaven. Thus we were encouraged to believe that although God promised to be in us and with us as individuals, (Jn. 17:23) and that he would never leave us, (Heb. 13:5), his promise was not based on his grace and unconditional love for us. Rather, we had a part to play in ensuring that he was faithful, and as a result could feel proud, singled out for his special attention and deserving of his visit.

Secondly, and more importantly, the heightened emotion and excitement of the worship was taken as a sign that God had 'shown up', an expression often used, and that his presence was a divine sanction, a *carte blanche* for the leaders to continue running the show as it was. This had been the very seat of my anxiety. Here was I, wrestling with what I was beginning to suspect was an abusive organisation, led by a group of people who were beginning to look like experts in the art of control and manipulation, adept at muscling their way in between me and my Father. But everything and everybody was telling me that God was here to demonstrate his approval of their beliefs and practices. If God was happy with the proceedings, who was I to complain? It was a powerful argument, with an intoxicating mixture of half truths and speculation.

As we have seen, there was an obsession with authority at the heart of the shepherding movement, a fixation with control that could reach into every corner of your life. Even the members' personal finances were not exempt. And so tithing was taught and strictly enforced – if you didn't agree to it, you couldn't get in! But they went further. Members were considered to be tithing only when a tenth of their income was paid to the Fellowship.

Many commentators believe that tithing as taught in Scripture has no relevance to Christians and that it was not a feature of the early church. Hastings's *Dictionary of the Apostolic Church*[12] states, 'it is admitted universally that the payment of tithes, or the tenths of possessions for sacred purposes, did not find a place in the Christian church during the age of the apostles and their immediate successors.' Other sources, including *The Encyclopedia Americana*,[13] agree that tithing was not practised in the early Christian church, but only became common by the sixth century.

Therefore, while the Bible teaches Christians to give, it does not teach tithing. Jake Barnett writes:

> Our proclivity to teach tithing is just one aspect of our tendency to prefer rules to freedom. But the New Testament concept of giving is so beautiful that it is difficult to understand why we resort to legalism. It appears that we feel God made a mistake in this area, and fear that our churches would suffer financial difficulty if we followed the Biblical pattern.[14]

It is yet another man-made rule, perhaps designed to validate us withholding 90 per cent rather than parting with 10 per cent. On a number of occasions, I've heard Tony Campolo making this point by singing his version of the little chorus *All to Jesus I Surrender*. He sang, '10 per cent to Jesus I surrender, 10 per cent to him I freely give'. The inference in the notion of tithing is this: I give God his slice, therefore I can do whatever I like with the rest. But that is to miss the point; it suggests that we can be trusted with our finances better than God can.

Here was an astonishing instance of a central doctrine of the church being built upon a couple of obscure verses of Scripture; another example of the Bible being called in to support an ideology. And here is the biblical authentication of the doctrine of tithing as taught in the shepherding movement: Melchizedek blessed Abram, and Abram gave to Melchizedek one tenth of all he possessed, (Gen. 14:18–20). That's it.

On that basis alone members were required to give one tenth of their gross income to the River of Life Fellowship, and we would be called upon to give offerings as well. Anything given to any other work, outreach or mission didn't count. Furthermore, because Abram gave to the one who blessed him, so we were required to give to the work of God's kingdom exclusively via the source of our blessing, our shepherds, for the elders to do with as they wished, without any accountability.

What increasingly worried me, and became one of the final, final straws that broke my camel's back was this twist: the source of my blessing, my spiritual nourishment, was to be my shepherd and him alone. No one else was to be trusted to speak into my life, apart from those who were higher up the hierarchy than my shepherd. If I had swallowed this, as I never fully could but many if not most did, I would be sealed into an incestuous little group, outside of which I could neither serve, receive, nor give. And that to me is spiritual death.

Spiritual abuse is a continuum that ranges from the mild and almost imperceptible to the mad extremes of the Branch Davidian that led to the deaths of nineteen men, thirty-four women, twenty-three children and four ATF agents in April 1993 in Waco, Texas. But the 'mild and almost imperceptible' may begin with an apparently benign rule for a woman to wear her hat and for a man to wear his Sunday suit in church. The danger is, firstly, it's a rule that is man-made and enforceable. Paul never taught the wearing of hats as a law, for in 1 Corinthians 11:15 he referred to a woman's hair as her covering, not a hat. Furthermore he claimed it was a 'custom', as translated in the NLT or a 'practice' in the NIV. But secondly, it's a rule that can begin to dilute the intimacy in our relationship with God – 'You have to be on your best behaviour and wear your Sunday best when you go to see him.' That's the sanctimonious thinking that Jesus set about dismantling when he told us we could call our heavenly Father 'Abba' – Daddy. In the Jewish tradition, they scrupulously avoided even mentioning his name, apart from once a year when the High Priest said it on the Day of Atonement, in hushed tones.

Rules as apparently innocuous as ladies' hats and gentlemen's Sunday suits can become building blocks in an organisational structure that hijacks God and restricts him to a geographical location. They can encourage the belief that God inhabits the 'the sanctuary' in some special way, so you have to go there to meet with him, and also, he's only around on a Sunday. Watch out when the preacher opens in prayer by saying, 'Let's come into the Lord's presence,' for either he hasn't thought things through or he really does believe that God lives in the church building – and only the church building.

That may be no more than lazy thinking, nonetheless it can create a flabby faith that leaves you desolate from Monday to Saturday. True faith is rich and relevant and meaningful, for it rests on God's promise that he lives and breathes in us every moment of every day. He wants to share in our challenges and disappointments, our failures and victories, our joys and our sadness.

Paul the apostle describes Christians as 'the temple of the living God,' (2 Cor. 6:16): the place where he lives. And Peter says, 'You are living stones that God is building into his spiritual home' (1 Pet. 2:5). It is a cruel lie therefore to tell people that the Christian faith revolves exclusively around our religious activities, or that the only meaningful way in which we can encounter him is when we are involved in some religious activity. God wants to be fully engaged with us in all of our daily doings.

The teaching that God inhabits the 'the sanctuary' in some special way drives a wedge between the common man and a God who desperately wants to have fellowship with his children. And because the leaders assume an incontrovertible position of authority in the sanctuary, they therefore believe that they are endowed with a unique relationship with God that places them in a position in which they are thought to be unaccountable and above scrutiny. This is far removed from the Bible model of church as described by Paul in his letter to the Ephesians. The job of the pastor/teacher is not to browbeat the flock into some sort of homogeneous group that believes without question exactly what they want them to believe or even what their denomination believes. The leader's responsibility is to '. . . equip God's people to do his work and build up the church, the body of Christ' (Eph. 4:12). The body of Christ is an organism: alive and growing, fulfilling and exciting to be part of in an empty, aimless world.

In reality, however, what often happens is that the leaders create a dependency culture that leads to spiritual obesity, and then they feed fat sheep who sit around grumbling, getting fatter and achieving nothing for the kingdom of heaven.

My wife and I brought a lady to church with us one Sunday evening – we both wished we hadn't. Her marriage was about to end. The next day her divorce would be final, and she was an emotional basket case. She accompanied us in the hope that she might find some crumb of comfort there, that God might intervene in her sad life, or that something might be said to help her make some sense of the cruelty of it all. The sermon was good and the worshipful music uplifting, but it was customary in that church for some to remain behind for a further time of singing after the formal part of the service. So in due course the minister stood up and said in a half whisper, 'The service is now over, but some of us are staying for a while longer. Those of you who must leave God's presence now, please do so quietly' – and the singing continued.

'Those of you who must leave God's presence . . .' What sort of a message did that send to our friend who teetered on the brink of even deeper depths of despair, having just been told that she must face her week of torment alone? To give the minister the benefit of the doubt, his unfortunate comment may have been an innocent slip of the tongue, but it didn't come from a vacuum. No, it sprang from a mind that believes that the church building is God's house – the place where he lives exclusively. Most emphatically it is not. The word 'church' as it appears in the New Testament never referred to a building, indeed for Christians there were no church buildings until the middle of the fourth century. The word 'church' refers to a community of people who have been 'called out'[15] and are recognised by God as 'a chosen people. You are a kingdom of priests, God's holy nation, his very own possession' (1 Pet. 2:9).

The final method that was used to keep the sheep inside the fold was driven by a misunderstanding that led to the misuse of one of the gifts of the Spirit. A central tenet of the shepherding movement was the belief that

God can speak directly into our lives through someone with the gift of prophecy (1 Cor. 12:10 and 28). Now there is no doubt that God can, and sometimes does speak to us in this way, however we were taught that God's word can come to us in either of two specific ways: the *rhéma* or the *lógos*. The belief was that the *rhéma* is God's specific word pertaining to a specific situation at a specific time, that is spoken directly into our lives by someone with a proven prophetic gifting. The *lógos* was said to be the collective body of his word available to us in the Bible.

The distinction between the two, however, is unclear. Indeed there are those who argue that the terms can be used interchangeably. *The Evangelical Dictionary of Biblical Theology*[16] for example, regards *lógos* and *rhéma* as synonyms, both equivalent to the same Hebrew word. However, relying on a number of other sources, including Vine's *Expository Dictionary of New Testament Words*,[17] we see that many commentators agree that *rhéma* can be defined as 'what has been uttered by the living voice', while the term *lógos* often suggests the written word, though not always.

Yet another commentator, Paul Arthur-Worsop, believes that the two words have vastly different meanings. He argues, '*Rhéma* stands at one end of the spectrum and *lógos* at the other. There is a large overlap between the meanings of the two words but the emphasis of *rhéma* is more to the mechanistic end of the spectrum whilst that of *lógos* is more to the spiritual end.' No doubt the truth lies somewhere in the middle.

Therefore, while it is not appropriate to conduct an in-depth study at this point, what has been established is that it is an intensely complicated topic. So why is it that in the River of Life Fellowship, and other related groups, there was such a dogmatic and over-simplistic belief in two discrete categories: the written word and the spoken word? Possibly because it suited the ideology of the community. As if to reinforce these two distinct categories, it was almost always the case that so-called prophetic utterances were prefixed and suffixed by the words, 'Thus saith the Lord . . .' For Christians who can sometimes be spiritually lethargic, preferring the quick fix of listening rather than diligently searching the Scriptures in pursuit of wisdom and guidance, whatever was sandwiched between prefix and suffix was by definition a '*rhéma* word' and therefore eagerly digested. You don't have to travel down that road very far until you begin to see the spoken word as being more relevant, certainly more accessible than the written word, with theological probity taking second place. A firm grasp of the whole Bible is therefore redundant, and the work of the abusive manipulator continues unimpeded.

# CHAPTER 8

# THE CASE OF THE RECOVERING SHEPHERD

Fourteen years had passed, almost to the day, since I had met Daniel in a little café near my home and he had told me, 'When you leave, they kill you.' And although through the years I have come to understand how and why, only now did I see that he was speaking from personal experience. He too had suffered greatly, having squeezed through his bars to freedom only a couple of years before I did.

Now we sit in his office discussing the early manuscripts of *Savage Shepherds*. We talk about tithing, the shepherds in their 'God's bankers' garb lined across the front of the church building collecting cheques and cash from the sheep, and he buries his head in his hands and groans, 'Did we really do that to you Adam?' But as we talk, it emerges that Daniel was as much a reluctant shepherd as I had been a reluctant sheep. There was much we had in common. Something had held him too, almost against his will. The only difference between us was that he was a leader and I was one of the led. The principle was the same.

Daniel and Tom met at university and had become close friends. It was in the early days of The Troubles in

Ireland, and Daniel believed that prayer could bring about healing in the land. To him, the promise in Bible was relevant:

> . . . if my people who are called by my name will humble themselves and pray and seek my face and turn from their wicked ways, I will hear from heaven and will fogive their sins and heal their land' (2 Chr. 7:14).

Daniel thought, 'If somebody would just do this, The Troubles might stop,' so he and Tom began to pray that God would intervene and bring healing to Ireland. But his Evangelical Protestant upbringing had taught him '. . . most Christians don't pray enough, don't try hard enough, don't read their Bibles enough, haven't enough faith, haven't repented enough, don't do anything right – it's a wonder that God will still let us into his heaven.' As a result, when his years of prayer made no obvious impact on the violence in his homeland, he says, 'I gave up a bit'. He concluded, 'It's clear that we're in trouble. Things are falling apart here because God doesn't like the state of the church, hasn't much time for Christians, and we're all under his judgement.'

Then in 1973, Daniel was given a tape recording of a sermon by Derek Prince on the topic of prayer. This was different: the teaching was unique and exciting. Derek taught that as Christians we have the spiritual power to overcome: we don't have to go through life as losers; we don't always have to live in defeat; we don't have to grovel and plead with God to do something that he has already commissioned and empowered us to do; and we don't have to go to church every Sunday to confess what miserable sinners we are. This was a breath of fresh air for both Daniel and Tom.

Daniel was desperate, so he wrote to Derek Prince saying that if he could give him just half an hour of his time, he would fly from Ireland to Florida to meet him. But Derek had planned a conference in London in June of the following year and he invited Daniel and Tom to meet him there. And so it was that they had lunch with Derek and Lydia Prince in London. They told Derek how much they valued the clarity and conviction of his teaching and that they needed more. Derek was helpful and promised to introduce them to two men whom he said could be trusted to plug them into all the different aspects of his teaching.

A year later they met these two men in America – one in Kansas and the other in East Lansing, Michigan. But they were quickly disillusioned. One was an erratic character with little or no organisational or pastoral skills, and questionable morality. The other was an extremely demanding person, authoritarian and impossible to please – he was going to be hard work. In addition, Daniel was unsure about some of the principles underlying the shepherding movement to which they were being introduced, although Tom appeared to be less hesitant. Daniel had other doubts as well – about Tom. He had always admired him as an honourable, godly man, but there were some aspects of his character that he was becoming unsure about. There was a single-mindedness about Tom that bordered on fanaticism, yet there was also an aura about him. He gave the impression that he had an inside track to God. He seemed to be more in tune with what God was doing in the world than anyone else was. He studied more, prayed more, fasted more and was incredibly focused. So regardless of his instincts, Daniel was prepared to set his concerns aside in the belief that, 'If one of us wrong, it's likely to be me.'

Signing up to the shepherding movement would be a big step, but while they were thinking and praying about it, along came Bret, and everything changed. Bret was a member of a related fellowship in another part of Ireland, and he opened a chasm between the two friends. He believed that every Christian on the face of the earth had demons from which they needed deliverance. Tom and Brenda had received deliverance under his ministry, and Tom's knee-jerk conclusion was that everybody in the Fellowship must have this same freedom from demon possession – including Daniel!

Daniel was unconvinced but he went along with it. 'Tom believes this stuff, so let's give it a shot,' he thought. However, nothing happened. No demons came out or even manifested themselves, and the predictable perception was that Daniel had a serious problem. Bret had identified demons of Lust and Unbelief among others in Daniel, but they were deep-seated, so deep-seated that even after several attempts to remove them they remained firmly entrenched – that was the verdict. But Bret also believed that demons can jump from one person to another, like a viral infection. One can only imagine how this made Daniel's new wife feel – they had been married less than a year at this point, 'And,' says Daniel, 'she began to wonder what on earth she had married.'

Daniel's 'demon possession' was creating a bad situation that simply had to be dealt with, and because of Daniel's respect for Derek Prince, he proposed to Tom that Derek's right-hand men should arbitrate; 'Do I have demons or do I not and what's to be done about it?'

By this time, however, the chap in Kansas had been run out of town. He was indeed, in Daniel's words, a 'nutcase', so two new men from the upper echelons of the shepherding movement in the US were asked to arbitrate. Bret was immediately exposed as a fraud and removed from the equation, and Daniel was instantly off the hook. 'I started over with a completely clean slate,' he says with a sigh. 'I was vindicated and my wife was apologetic.' However, part of the package was that he and Tom would now embrace Derek's representatives as their shepherds to protect them from another Bret-type episode, the first having exposed their spiritual immaturity. It quickly became apparent to Daniel that these new shepherds were more concerned with their position of absolute power atop the network of related fellowships than they were for the people under their care. But with Derek Prince appearing to sanction the relationship, he continued to suppress his hesitations and went along with it.

When Derek renounced the shepherding movement in 1983, he was seen by some of the other Fort Lauderdale leaders to be taking a sideways step. They were convinced that God was launching a major 'latter day' initiative in the world, in Europe in particular, but Derek, by then approaching seventy, was thought to be too old. They decided they would allow him to slide off the radar with a degree of dignity. Their view was that he was missing God's best, paddling his own canoe, '. . . but God will look after him, and might still use him to help a few people.' History has demonstrated just how wrong they were: Derek's ministry went from strength to strength.

The departure of such a central and high-profile character as Derek called for a new initiative to maintain momentum. The response was a call for a fresh approach to accountability and, typically, Tom rose to the challenge by becoming increasingly intense. He required every shepherd in the River of Life Fellowship to be answerable to him for every detail of their lives: finances,

family and relationships. In addition, each sheep was to
be similarly accountable to his shepherd. The atmosphere in the church became even more pressured.

It quickly became apparent that the call to a new
level of intensity had created a potentially explosive
situation, and Daniel took an initiative to release the
building pressure by requesting a meeting of the top
brass of the shepherding movement. It took place in
Washington DC. His view was that the people needed
to be freed from the oppressive demand for absolute
submission, and it was agreed that there was indeed
room for a degree of freedom of choice. Also, and cru-
cially, if some of the men in the River of Life Fellowship
wanted to 'switch allegiance', to choose Daniel's less
demanding style of leadership, they must be allowed to
do so. This was an astonishing turn-around that effectively turned a fundamental teaching on its head. It
was more than a mere topic for debate; it went way
beyond issues of loyalty and trust. It was a critical issue
of principle: if it is God who places the shepherd in a
position of delegated authority in the life of the sheep,
how can a mere sheep be trusted to choose his shepherd?

There followed what Daniel describes as the worst three
or four months of his life. He believed that the shepherd's
role in the lives of the 'flock that God has entrusted' to
him was to care for them. Most were stressed out of their
heads, some were in deep depression and needed counselling, but Tom was so self-obsessed that he refused to
take time to visit any of them. 'If they need me, they know
where I am,' was the nearest Tom ever appeared to get to
an understanding of practical pastoral care.

As a result there emerged what Daniel saw as a subtle
perversion that confirmed his worst fears: the people

were becoming secondary to the ministry in direct contrast to Peter's model for leadership:

> Care for the flock of God entrusted to you. Watch over it willingly, not grudgingly – not for what you will get out of it, but because you are eager to serve God. Don't lord it over the people assigned to your care, but lead them by your good example (1 Pet. 5:2,3).

To Tom, spiritual responsibility was a burden that was heavier to carry than just about anything else. Consequently, the weight and importance of the burden carried by a shepherd justified the accumulation of resources around him – people whose responsibility it became to wash his car, grease his skis, do his housework, tend his garden – all in the name of releasing the shepherd to rest in the Spirit, to hear from God, to lead the flock, and to read his newspaper.

The pressure was so intense that Tom needed regular holidays, taking, on average, one every six weeks. 'But what about the men?' implored Daniel. 'They're falling apart. If you need all these breaks, does that not suggest that they need one as well? If the strategy is so stressful, could it be that it's the wrong strategy?' The reply was predictable: 'That's not what the members are telling me, and anyway, I'm different. I carry the responsibility for the spiritual well-being of them all. My burden is heavy.' And so it seemed that neither Tom nor any of the other leaders knew anything about Jesus' promise 'For my yoke fits perfectly, and the burden I give you is light' (Mt. 11:30).

Nor did it appear that Tom was interested in whether or not the people were getting anything out of his teaching. He had been preaching for a solid year on a single chapter of the Bible. The members were getting bored, and some of them suggested that a little variety might be a good idea – something from the New Testament, perhaps. But that was not Tom's concern. It didn't much matter that they didn't like it, nor did the fact that they were not benefiting from it. All that mattered to Tom was his obsession with the challenge of wringing every drop of truth and meaning from that particular Scripture.

Many abusers have the spectacular gift of an encyclopaedic memory, and Tom was no different. He could call up incidents that most people had long forgotten. Fragments of conversations and comments in minute detail would be hurled with great accuracy to undermine, humiliate, accuse and destroy – a technique that could reduce grown men to tears. The eloquence with which he could preach was matched by an ability to tongue-lash his victims, and Daniel, who had loved and trusted him, was systematically torn to shreds. Tom interpreted Daniel's willingness to listen to the people and his efforts to free them from oppression as an attempted insurrection. In Tom's view, Daniel's response to those who spoke to him about their life's concerns and woes should have been, 'It's inappropriate for you to talk to me about those issues. They are between you and your shepherd.' Daniel was resisting this form of control, on the sheep's behalf.

Each sheep was seen as an extension of his specific shepherd. A shepherd would want his sheep to do well, to tow the line, follow the rules, be obedient, have an idyllic family life and be financially successful. The shepherd would be heavily invested in his sheep because their success ultimately reflected the quality of his leadership. On the other hand, no shepherd liked his sheep to have unresolved questions in his life. That would be taken as evidence of the shepherd's inability to hear from God on the sheep's behalf and to answer all his questions. But this all-encompassing relationship would be jeopardised if the discrete line of communication between sheep and shepherd was interrupted or tampered with.

Tom's way of dealing with problem people was to stand aloof from them – 'If you befriend them,' he argued, 'they will think everything is OK. You must distance yourself and they'll get the message that there's a problem to be dealt with.' In his view, alienating the sheep would send them scurrying to their shepherd in utter humility, reinforcing the significance of the shepherd's position in their lives. The shepherd would never seek out the sheep, never be proactive.

With this degree of insight into Tom's *modus operandi*, I could more easily understand why certain hymn writers were recruited to support his view of how church should be run. Clearly, Tom believed that when God's people disappoint him, he would withdraw until the erring child cried out:

> Return, O holy Dove, return,
> Sweet messenger of rest;
> I hate the sins that made thee mourn,
> And drove thee from my breast.[18]

This was a classic example of using a religious model to support a dubious strategy. The unthinking or immature sheep who might be struggling with doubts about their community's beliefs and practices would be intimidated, not only by the leader's 'strong devotion, humility and severe bodily discipline' (Col. 2:23), but also by a venerated hymn writer who's been brought on board for them to deal with. And there are few people who are sufficiently free-spirited and strong to resist succumbing to such potent personalities.

Daniel, by contrast, chose to draw close to the sheep, to show love and acceptance following the example of the parable of the lost sheep (Mt. 18:12,13). Tom saw this as a threat to his life's work, indeed his high calling and at the Washington meeting, he believed Daniel had committed the cardinal sin of manipulating the most senior leaders so that they came down on his side, those to whom he should be submissive and obedient.

Tom and Daniel both knew that the remaining shepherds of Fort Lauderdale were extremely sensitive to any tension between the leaders of what they regarded as their missionary outpost. The River of Life Fellowship was strategically important to their European evangelistic project, and since Daniel had exploited that sensitivity, their disagreement reached a new intensity.

The deep corruption at the heart of the principles underlying the shepherding movement was becoming more apparent. Derek Prince's analysis was right: selfish ambition had taken over. The sheep were there to serve the shepherds and to enhance their status, just as Ezekiel had prophesied six hundred years BC: 'Though you were my shepherds, you didn't search for my sheep when they were lost. You took care of yourselves and left the sheep to starve' (Ezek. 34:8). The shepherds directly above Daniel in the chain of command, cared little about the welfare of the people.

Daniel's close involvement with the shepherding movement had lasted around ten years. For perhaps three of those years he was convinced that if anyone really wanted to be at the front-line of the action, in a vibrant, growing, relevant church making a difference in the world, this was the place to be. To be out from under the covering of the shepherding movement was to settle

for second best, to be content with the thin end of
Christianity. But now the stark contrast between his and
Tom's reaction to the suffering of their people led to
Daniel's disillusionment with the shepherding movement. A narcissistic obsession with themselves as God's
anointed leaders of the work of the Lord had replaced
the early selfless commitment to the Lord of the work.

To Tom, there was no gain without pain. To Daniel,
the example of the Good Shepherd was that 'He lets me
rest in green meadows; he leads me beside peaceful
streams' (Ps. 23:2). Under the gruelling pressure of
accountabil-ity, obedience, serving, tithing and submission to authority, there were neither green meadows nor
peaceful streams. Tom believed that God made his children feel isolated and convicted when they got it wrong,
and so the shepherds should treat the sheep in the same
way. To Daniel, it was important to seek out the wan-
dering lamb, to show him love and acceptance, no
apportionment of guilt, and no condemnation. Their
approaches had become so diametrically opposed that
there was no longer any possibility of reconciliation or
compromise – none. And so the die was cast; Daniel left
and was isolated and walked much the same path as I
did two years later.

There was no ruined business and no police investigation in his case, but he suffered in the same lonely
wilderness as I did. Tom's behaviour appeared to be vindicated; God was taking over from where he had left off.
Daniel was finished, without hope, out from under the
covering, rejected by God and heading for damnation.
His downward trajectory might not have been as dramatic as mine, but it was no less complete.

As Daniel and I talked, a decade and a half after the
torrents of abuse had subsided, it was clear that the

similarities in our experiences, pre-Shepherding, during Shepherd-ing and post-Shepherding, were striking. The gulf between us in terms of our status within the organisation had been as wide as it could get: Daniel functioned at the dizzy heights of strategy meetings and social gatherings with the Fort Lauderdale Five and their families, I never made it beyond the first rung of the ladder. But the single common factor was the effect of a hierarchy that created an elite group of people whose influence it was difficult to defy. If you were not prepared to play the game, it would crush you.

Can we protect ourselves from such manipulation, bearing in mind that it is made possible by human failings in both abused and abuser? Do we build a fence around ourselves to keep potentially harmful people at bay, deflecting all attempts to engage with us at an intimate level? No we don't, for we must love, and we cannot love from behind a wall.

We may never be in a position where we can say that we are impervious to abuse, whichever side of the desk we sit behind – abuser or abused. But we can come to an understanding of what the Bible actually teaches about leadership. A good understanding of Ezekiel's pronouncements against the shepherds, as we shall see next, his foretelling of the coming of the Good Shepherd and then the announcement by Jesus that he, the Good Shepherd had come and would be a Prince among us, should expose as deceitful, any attempt, by anyone, ever, to take up an exalted position in the life of another, or to afford another person an exalted position. That is our best defence.

# CHAPTER 9

# ABUSE-PROOF YOUR RELATIONSHIPS

Abusive leadership is nothing new. The prophet Ezekiel, whose name means 'God strengthens', verbally lacerated the shepherds of his day and brought to them the devastating word of the Lord: 'I now consider these shepherds my enemies, and I will hold them responsible for what has happened to my flock. I will take away their right to feed the flock, along with their right to feed themselves. I will rescue my flock from their mouths; the sheep will no longer be their prey' (Ezek. 34:10).

What the Lord was saying through Ezekiel to sheep who had been downtrodden and exploited by those who were supposed to care for them, is as relevant today as it was 2,500 years ago: 'In this way, they will know that I, the LORD their God, am with them . . . You are my people, and I am your God, says the Sovereign LORD' (Ezek. 34:30–31). The full impact of that amazing truth may never fully penetrate minds that have been dulled by the religious mindset that promotes the model of a hierarchical family of God. But the notion that those with theological degrees and titles, self-appointed shepherds have 'an inside track to God' is destroyed as God bypasses the shepherds with the words, 'You are my people, and I am your God.'

It is beyond doubt that the single most significant key, not only in the process of recovery from spiritual abuse but also in abuse-proofing your relationship to faith, is a firm understanding of grace and mercy. Grace is getting what you don't deserve: mercy is not getting what you do deserve, I was vulnerable because I had no real understanding of either.

As we have already seen, the savage shepherd is skilled, consciously or otherwise, in exploiting the greatest of all human needs after food, clothing and shelter: acceptance. Now that might be human acceptance or it might be our Father's acceptance, but because the teaching from Fort Lauderdale at that time, underpinning the shepherding movement, was so deeply embedded in the psyche of the shepherds *and* the sheep, there was no discernible distinction between man's approval and God's approval.

To reiterate, the sheep were taught that their attitude toward those whom God had set in 'delegated authority' over them was the outward and visible expression of their attitude toward God himself. Therefore, in the eyes of the sheep, God took on many forms, indeed as many forms as the shepherd had moods. God might be laid back and liberal, or morose and capricious. If the shepherd had had a bad day, or was ill, or had a hangover, then the sheep might get mauled when they needed a gentle embrace or an encouraging word. Or the sheep might experience the 'rough edge of God's tongue' because the shepherd had had a row with his wife. In other words, the Fort Lauderdale decree, for that's what it was, focused exclusively on the attitude of the sheep while it totally ignored the fact that shepherds had human failings too.

Fear lay at the root of life in a shepherding community: fear of rejection. It used to be said that Tom had the rare ability to preach for an hour on grace and still you went home feeling guilty and condemned. On the face of it, everything we did in the River of Life Fellowship was with a view to pleasing God. We fasted, we prayed, we had so many meetings that we had meetings to arrange meetings. We had home group meetings, home group leaders' meetings. We had all-night prayer meetings and early morning prayer meetings. But the reality was that life was a series of external activities aimed at placating a grumpy God and his sidekicks, the shepherds.

Then one day a friend came from Edmonton, Alberta to visit my family, and I asked if he would address our home group meeting. Rowan worked as an Air Traffic Controller and was a part-time pastor of a church in his home town. He spoke of the grace of God in a way that I'd never heard before. The air that was contaminated with conditions, with 'Ifs' and 'Buts' and 'Maybes', suddenly became as clear as the driven snow with the simplicity of Romans 8:1: 'So now there is no condemnation for those who belong to Christ Jesus. For the power of the life-giving Spirit has freed you through Christ Jesus from the power of sin that leads to death.' Wonderful stuff!

Rowan reminded us that every one of Paul's, Peter's, James's and Jude's New Testament letters contain the greeting, 'Grace and peace to you,' or reference was made to the 'gospel of grace'. Grace, therefore, defined as God's undeserved favour, was central to the gospel.

As Rowan expounded the simple message of God's total, unconditional and extravagant love for us, my heart began to beat a little faster. Here was perhaps the first person I'd ever met who appeared to believe what I had come to believe: God is not a police officer, always poised to club us over the head when we get it wrong, and that we do not have to achieve his high standards in order for him to love and accept us as his own.

Our eyes widened in wonder as he preached, 'There is nothing you can do to make him love you more, and there is nothing you can do to make him love you less. Satan is the accuser of the brethren, not God!' That was revolutionary. All my life I had been taught that it was God who constantly stood in judgement over me. What a dreadful lie had been thrust on me by the fundamentalism of my youth!

And then Rowan quoted from Galatians 5: 'For if you are trying to make yourselves right with God by keeping the law, you have been cut off from Christ! You have fallen away from God's grace.' All at once I could see that my years in an oppressive regime had formed within me a version of grace that was a grotesque distortion of what it truly is. All of my Christian life, I had been trying to earn God's grace and the favour of callous manipulators, when all the while I was alienating myself from Christ, I was falling away from grace.

But the odd thing was that a number of those in our home group that evening left and never returned. They were being offered the opportunity to think for themselves, to evaluate, to weigh up the beliefs and practices of their church against the startling truths of the Scriptures. And they turned away. In a sense they did what Paul the apostle talked about in his letter to the Romans: 'Instead of believing what they knew was the truth about God, they deliberately chose to believe lies' (Rom. 1:25).

We live in a meritocratic world that has conditioned us to believe that we always get what we deserve. If we work hard, we get rewarded. If we do not work hard, we will suffer. It's built into our genes. I live in the North of Ireland where the education system still operates the grammar school/secondary school selection procedure in the primary schools, although it's in the process of changing. When my oldest son was sitting his transfer test to decide his educational future he was only eleven. I thought I would encourage him by offering an incentive. 'If you pass this test,' I told him, 'we'll go to London for a weekend.' Instantly I recognised that I was also saying the same thing another way around: 'Boy, if you don't pass your exam, we'll not be going anywhere!' That's meritocracy and it's horrible, and so I told him we'd go either way, when all the fuss of the exams had died down.

Grace runs counter to every fibre of our human nature, particularly in terms of our relationship with God. We just do not like to be told that we have nothing to bring to that relationship other than a humble and a contrite heart, that there is nothing we can contribute to our salvation – it's all of grace.

This was indelibly carved into my mind on one occasion when I was the guest speaker at a men's conference deep in rural Ireland. The delegates were senior lay people from a range of denominations, but mainly Presbyterians. There were church elders, retired ministers and some still serving, and there was an old fellow who had been principal of a Bible college in Canada.

Feeling slightly mischievous toward the end of the last day I prepared some questions and had them printed on pieces of paper – quite spontaneously. The key question I wanted them to address was, 'Define in 15–20 words what it means to fall from grace.' I had the question papers handed out at the end of one of the sessions to be collected at the beginning of the next.

I did a quick analysis of the answers, ignoring the other questions – they were dummies – and then I asked if we could agree that a fair summary of all the answers was that to fall from grace is for a Christian to return to a life of sin. All agreed; that was a fair summary. I was

surprised by the answers, for these men, some of them
with a significantly better formal theological education
than I had, had all missed the point. How many times
had they read Galatians chapter 5? Hundreds of times?
Thousands of times? Some I'm sure had even preached
with conviction from it, and yet a couple of them almost
fell off their seats when I rejected their answers by saying, 'Falling from grace does not involve doing bad
things. On the contrary, it involves doing good things –
observing the law – for the wrong reason.' And when the
sharp intakes of breath and the mumblings of 'Heresy!'
had subsided, I read that wonderful Scripture in
Galatians 5: 'For if you are trying to make yourselves
right with God by keeping the law, you have been cut off
from Christ! You have fallen away from God's grace.'

You do not fall from grace by keeping the law, you fall
from grace if you think that God will love you more if you
do; that's the essence of it. Now isn't that as plain as the
nose on your face? And wouldn't you think it inconceiv-
able that those men could have read that life-giving
Scripture and missed its meaning? But this was my learning curve. Having been taught a doctrine, and then having
built their belief system around it, they were not prepared
to dismantle it, even when they saw something in
Scripture that contradicted it – that's a human tendency.
That's the power of the paradigm, and it's what had happened to my dad's old friend Andrew. He had been
taught, and had taught the Scriptures all of his adult life,
for fifty years or more, but he preferred to live in varying
degrees of darkness, and share his shades of grey with others rather than allow the light of Scriptures to challenge
the dogma of his denomination and set him free. And the
reason is that a man's denomination is part of his identity.

Jesus touched on this when he said to the Pharisees,
'You search the Scriptures because you think they give

you eternal life. Yet you refuse to come to me to receive this life' (Jn. 5:39–40). There is no doubt that some of the Pharisees and teachers of the law knew that Jesus was their Messiah, but he was the wrong type of Messiah. He was messy, he didn't conform, he rocked boats, asked awkward questions, he changed things and he disregarded their paradigms, he kicked over tables, literally and metaphorically. What respectable church leader would want someone so out-of-the-box as that in their congregation, let alone want to follow him?

Nicodemus was a Pharisee and a member of the Sanhedrin. The Sanhedrin was the highest Jewish assembly for government in the New Testament era. When Nicodemus came to see Jesus he said, 'Rabbi, we all know that God has sent you to teach us. Your miraculous signs are evidence that God is with you' (Jn. 3:2). The title 'Rabbi' was a respectful term applied by the Jews to their spiritual instructors. Make no mistake, they knew who Jesus was.

The Jews had been in the waiting mode for over four thousand years. Every time a Levite slaughtered a lamb to make atonement for the sins of the people, every time a scapegoat was driven into the desert with the sins of the people on its head, it was a reminder that one day their promised Redeemer would come. The slaughtered lamb was the symbol John the Baptist had in mind when he saw Jesus and cried out, 'Look! There is the Lamb of God, who takes away the sin of the world!' (Jn. 1:29).

But the ritual had taken on a life and meaning of its own. It had become a comfortable end in itself rather than a means to an end. For the Pharisees to acknowledge that Jesus was heralding the end of an era would require them to accept that everything was about to change. Jesus, the carpenter's son from backwoods Nazareth was now the High Priest of the New

Covenant, and they simply could not accept the implications for their way of life and their position in society
– so they had him killed.

My wilderness experience had taught me to read the
Bible as though it was tomorrow morning's newspaper.
It was exciting, fresh and new. I discovered that I had
grown up with many profound and liberating truths
having been stood on their heads. Why? I suspect it is
religious people's way of controlling free-thinking people by keeping them in fear.

I grew up in a good Christian family. We all went to a
little Brethren Gospel Hall, where my five siblings and I
in turn surrendered our lives to Jesus. As I approached
my teenage years my father was justifiably concerned
that I might wander from the straight and narrow –
which in time I did, with a vengeance. He would often
beat me over the head with a text from Paul's letter to
the Colossians, 2:21: 'Don't handle, don't eat, don't
touch.' And he painted a picture of an angry God who
would wreak havoc in my life if I handled, tasted or
touched such things as wine, women and song, parties,
cinemas and dancing: even buying sweets or reading a
comic on the Sabbath were outlawed. And it worked –
for a while.

Fear kept me from those deadly sins, until one day
when I was in London on a business trip and I went into
a restaurant for lunch. It was my first such trip away
from home – I was only nineteen – and I thought I'd
have my first glass of Guinness to celebrate my Irishness
in a 'foreign land'. But I forgot it was Sunday. In my part
of Ireland in the late 1960s most shops and restaurants
closed to observe the Sabbath. And so I had committed
two cardinal sins: I had consumed alcohol and I had
bought it on a Sunday. However, since there was neither
thunderbolt to crack my skull nor pillar of fire to incin-

erate me, it wasn't long until I had discarded all the restraints that had hedged me in to that point.

The techniques of fear and the threat of violence are ineffective in controlling human behaviour, and the reason is this: we are instinctively rebellious. Place a number of toys on the floor in front of a child, explain that he can play with any of them 'apart from that one', and of course we all know which item the child will reach for as soon as your back is turned – even before your back is turned!

Paul said it – the law doesn't work. 'No one can ever be made right in God's sight by doing what his law commands. For the more we know God's law, the clearer it becomes that we aren't obeying it' (Rom. 3:20). And he elaborated: 'I would never have known that coveting [for example] is wrong if the law had not said, "Do not covet." But sin took advantage of this law and aroused all kinds of forbidden desires within me!' (Rom. 7:7,8). Allow me to paraphrase: 'Tell me not to do something, and that's the very thing I will want to do.'

Therefore, for most Christians who recognise the utter futility of trying to observe the law in its entirety, there are only two options: they either slide into self-deception or they give up even trying. I'm a pragmatist. I chose the latter, and from my twenties in the late sixties until my encounter with God that fateful day in November 1980 when he welcomed his prodigal back into his family, I lived a wild and profligate life.

Years later when spiritual abuse derailed my faith, or so it seemed – when all my points of reference had melted away; and when all I had was my Bible and the deep conviction that God loved me, although I had only a faint idea why or how much – I devoured my Bible in a frantic search to find something concrete on which to rebuild my life.

Religious people had failed me, but I was determined to find the kernel of truth that lay buried under thick sediments of tradition and empty ritual. In my search, I found many signs that God had not deserted me, nor ever would. I was enlightened and inspired almost daily by new revelations, and I was enthralled by the power and beauty of much that I was familiar with. But I found it deeply disturbing that religious men had totally misrepresented, consciously or otherwise it mattered not, many of Scripture's profound and liberating truths.

And my conclusion was this: if they have got something as explicit as the 'Do not handle, eat and touch' command wrong, could I rely on anything I had been taught? For Paul did indeed write to the Colossians and say, 'Don't handle, don't eat, don't touch'. But in my determined search for that kernel of truth, I discovered for the first time the significance of the whole text, for Paul did not write a couple of verses to the Christians in Colosse, he wrote them a letter, to be read as a letter.

While Paul was certainly not encouraging his readers to engage in questionable practices, it was the man-made rules, the 'human commands and teachings' he was telling them to avoid.

> You have died with Christ, and he has set you free from the evil powers of this world. So why do you keep on following the rules of the world, such as, 'Don't handle, don't eat, don't touch.' Such rules are mere human teachings about things that are gone as soon as we use them. These rules may seem wise because they require strong devotion, humility, and severe bodily discipline. But they have no effect when it comes to conquering a person's evil thoughts and desires (Col. 2:20–23).

Matthew Henry comments thus: 'Christians are freed by Christ from the ritual observances of Moses' law, and delivered from that yoke of bondage which God himself had laid upon them.'[19]

But still the question remains: why is a distorted version of the truth so often embraced and propounded? And why do men, who should know the extent of our freedom in Christ, insist on enforcing obsolete rules, or rules that are their own, pretending they're God's? Once again it's to do with the issues of freedom and control. To leaders of abusive churches, the suggestion that God loves his people totally, extravagantly and unconditionally is anathema, and while I can't be sure why that is, I suspect it's because they have an incomplete understanding of God's grace. There is much anecdotal evidence that abusers have often had troubled childhoods with unsatisfactory relationships with one or both parents. Many fall into that category. They have grown up with a view of God that is influenced by the nature and character of their earthly father who was remote, without affection and demanding.

Jack Frost, founder of Shiloh Place Ministries, is an example of a successful pastor whose ministry was radically transformed when, for the first time, God revealed a measure of the depth of his love for him. As a boy, Jack had longed for his father's approval and affection. He describes his background:

> I just wanted him to smile at me, or to say that he was proud to be my dad. Yet when I opened my heart to receive his love, I always was left empty and disappointed. I was now nineteen years old, yet I could not remember one time in my life when my dad had held me close, or said, 'I love you.' As a result of the rejection I felt, I had ceased being my father's son and never wanted to see him again.

But like so many men from his generation, Dad didn't
know how to express affection. He was a good man and
would have died for me. But to him, showing emotion
was a sign of weakness. Because he had grown up during the Great Depression, and lived in a fatherless home,
he built a fortress around his heart to protect himself
from pain. Then he went to war and learned even more
survival skills. Later, he expressed his love simply by
providing for his family financially, and by teaching his
two sons to survive in a merciless world. He always told
me, 'Never be weak by showing emotions or tears! Be
tough! Be a man!'[20]

And so, because the love of their earthly father was distorted, many spiritual abusers have at best a limited concept of unconditional love. They believe that they can
impress God with their 'strong devotion, humility and
severe bodily discipline' (Col.2:23) and when they look
around at their feeble sheep who exhibit none of these
virtues, they conclude that stern control and the restric-
tion of man-made rules will encourage them to rise to
the challenge.

The God of the abuser is an intolerant, demanding
God, who strikes fear into the hearts of his people, fear
that they will incur God's anger and punishment if they
don't conform to multiplying rules. And yet the apostle
John assures us: 'There is no fear in love. But perfect love
drives out fear, because fear has to do with punishment'
(1 Jn. 4:18 NIV).

Ken Blue's book *Healing Spiritual Abuse*[21] was crucial
to my recovery. It is based on Matthew 23, a chapter that
can contribute more to our understanding of both the
root of spiritual abuse and the techniques employed by
the abuser, than anything else you're ever likely to read.
The first thing Jesus said to the crowds and to his disci-

ples in that chapter was 'The teachers of religious law and the Pharisees are the official interpreters of the Scriptures' (verse 2). That was their job and their preoccupation, and yet Paul the apostle describes the law as 'our guardian and teacher to lead us until Christ came. So now, through faith in Christ, we are made right with God. But now that faith in Christ has come, we no longer need the law as our guardian' (Gal. 3:24,25).

And what is the message that Christ brings us? He gives us a new law to replace the Law of Moses: 'Love each other. Just as I have loved you, you should love each other' (Jn. 13:34). In another place, he demolished an expert in the law who tested him by asking, 'Which is the most important commandment in the law of Moses?' Jesus, rather than quoting one of the laws of Moses, replied, '"You must love the LORD your God with all your heart, all your soul, and all your mind." This is the first and greatest commandment. A second is equally important: "Love your neighbour as yourself."' And then he adds a most radical statement; 'All the other commandments and all the demands of the prophets are based on these two commandments' (Mt. 22:36–40). In other words, if you love God, your neighbour and yourself, then you will endeavour to keep the law, but it will be because you want to, not because you have to. Our relationship with law is therefore revolutionised; it becomes an internal principle, no longer an external code.

The next thing you'll see in Matthew 23 is Jesus' dislike of titles, or to be more specific, the special positions afforded to people with titles. And yet religious organisations and communities appear to have an obsession with titles – Reverend, Reverend Doctor, Pastor, Bishop, Canon, Father, Very Reverend – thereby totally ignoring the principle Jesus laid down: 'They love to sit at the head table at banquets and in the most prominent seats in the synagogue! They enjoy the attention they get on the streets, and they enjoy being called "Rabbi". Don't ever let anyone call you "Rabbi" . . .' And Jesus makes it clear why we are not to call anyone Rabbi, meaning 'my master': 'for you have only one teacher, and all of you are on the same level as brothers and sisters' (Mt. 23:6–8). In other words, as we have already established, there's no hierarchy in God's kingdom, for we are all equal. But isn't this another example of an unequivocal and radical teaching of Jesus being totally ignored? Religion has created its own hierarchy, for the same reason the Pharisees did – it ascribes status. And we love status!

Spiritual abuse is a continuum ranging from the mild, that's difficult to identify, to the most extreme form that leads people to lay down their lives in the face of an attack by 'Babylon', as one hundred men, women and children were prepared to do in Waco, Texas in 1993. So there may be many who will read this book and ask, 'But how do I know whether I'm in an abusive church?'

There's a number of telltale signs which we can look at in a moment, but the most important sign is always that where there's abuse, genuine love will be thin on the ground. However, we need to be careful to distinguish between godly love – *agape*, and human erotic love – *eros*.

John Powell, in his book, *Why am I Afraid to Love?*[22] says, 'Whatever else can and should be said about love, it is quite evident that true love demands self-forgetfulness.'

That's *agape* love, self-forgetful love, the love of the higher lifting up the lower, the love you see in a community that is based on mutual submission as taught by Peter (1 Pet. 5:5)[23]: a voluntary and reciprocal attitude of giving in, co-operating, assuming responsibility, and carrying a burden.

*Eros*, however, seeks in others the fulfilment of its own life's hunger. It is not God's love. For Jesus, in his great commandment said, 'love each other in the same way that I love you' (Jn. 15:12). Jesus was not calling us to love one another as much as he loves us, that would be unreasonable, and he's much too practical for that. But he wants us to love one another in the same way that he loves us, with *agape*, self-forgetful love.

Consider, for example, the concept of 'love bombing', a common technique employed by those seeking to gain control of another's mind. A young man, rejected or not understood by his parents, or as in my case, someone recovering from a life of depravity, becomes part of what turns out to be an abusive church. He is made to feel that he has 'come in from the cold', he is showered with love and attention, he is made to feel special, valued and accepted. But there's a hook, for as soon as he begins to ask awkward questions, or shows the least sign of free-thinking – invariably interpreted as a rebellious spirit – it is made abundantly clear to him that the love he has enjoyed and has grown to need is at risk of being withdrawn. That's *Eros* love: the abusers are seeking to fulfil their own life's hunger at the expense of others.

It is not difficult, therefore, to understand why many choose remain in an environment in which they are manipulated, controlled and exploited, when the alternative is more rejection.

To date I have resisted applying the word 'cult' directly to the River of Life Fellowship, and that's for a number of reasons. Firstly, the word has become overused, and its true meaning has become obscured and confused. It has become a catch-all for almost any social group, religious or otherwise, that's considered to be different from the norm, or not understood, or feared. Such groups can often be legitimate and harmless. For example, Christian communities are, or should be, different from the norm, and are often misunderstood, but that does not necessarily mean they are cults. It is therefore important to define as accurately as possible what a cult is, in order to compare it to the biblical model of church.

Any group, religious or otherwise, can be said to be a cult when it uses mind control techniques to deceive, to influence and to govern its followers. However, given the freedom Christians have in Christ, the activities of a Christian group or community become totally unacceptable when *any* attempt is made to exert *any* control for any reason.

In Christian cults or abusive churches the degree of control will vary in intensity but will usually include some, if not all, of the following:

- There will be some degree of control over the lifestyle and time of its members.
- There will be an attempt to dictate what its members should read, even eat and with whom they spend their 'off' time.
- Members will be discouraged from attending churches from other denominations.
- There will often be a claim, implicit or explicit, that the church or the group of churches or the movement the church belongs to has a monopoly of the truth.
- Members will often live together in groups, perhaps in communes, but not necessarily. You will often find them moving house to be close to each other or to their place of worship or centre of activities.
- Family and non-group associates will be shunned.
- The church will be built around a single charismatic character, a self-appointed leader with complete authority, usually a self-centred and self-seeking person.

- Members are taught not to question the teachings, practices, or ideas of the leader because they are 'God's anointed'.
- A member may not be told everything up front when joining the group. Instead, controlling ideas and restrictive demands will be drip-fed.
- The leader will always attract the attention and veneration of the members upon themselves. They will often be seen parading their piety.
- There will usually be a tendency to withhold truth from non-members. Members will be told and will believe that outsiders won't understand the practices of the group. There is often a suspicion of anything outside – not just the secular world, but all the rest of the churches.
- There is usually a system in place that controls or influences how the members spend their money. Tithing will be taught and enforced, but more, members will be required to tithe exclusively *to the group*. Anything given elsewhere doesn't count.

Most of the elements listed above could easily be identified in the shepherding movement with which I was familiar until the early nineties. It is not an exhaustive list, however, nor are its points limited to cults or what might be regarded as 'odd religious groups'. They are just some of the tools of the abusers' trade, a profession that knows no denominational boundaries as it works to create an unhealthy form of the basic ingredient of a normal community – group identity. An overly strong 'them and us' attitude enables the leaders to isolate the flock from outside influences and is unhealthy. It enables the abnormal to become the norm.

It is more productive to focus on the antibody, rather than becoming obsessed by the dissection and analysis of the viruses. Many people are bored by church life, there is nothing abnormal in that. However, if you recognise your church in the list above, if it makes you feel fear, guilt or condemnation, or if you are discouraged from interpreting Scripture for yourself under the guidance of the Holy Spirit, the Spirit of Truth whom Jesus promised will guide us into all truth, then it is your responsibility as a Christian to heed the warning lights. Stay clear!

For those for whom this warning has come too late, healing is available. But since spiritual abuse can leave its victims suspicious of any Christian input – as it did with me for several years – let me suggest a guaranteed method of treatment. Take your medicine three times a day, although please don't get legalistic about it!

The apostle John told us that God is love. Three times a day, read 1 Corinthians 13:4–7, replacing the word 'love' with the word 'God'. Many of us have had a bad experience with our earthly fathers, as we have seen from Jack Frost's story, and so there may be times when Christians refer to God as 'our heavenly Father' and negative images come to mind. But do this three times a day and you will soon find that our Father God is never angry, never accuses, never rejects, never leaves us to our own devices. He always loves, always forgives, is always faithful, is always loyal, and he will never, ever abuse his children. That's guaranteed!

## 1 Corinthians 13:4–7

> God is patient.
> God is kind.
> God does not envy.
> God does not boast.
> God is not self-seeking.

God is not easily angered.
God keeps no record of wrongs.
God does not delight in evil.
God rejoices in the truth.
God always protects.
God always perseveres.
God never fails.

Each day, Monday to Saturday, for two weeks, focus on one of these wonderful attributes. On Sunday, reflect on the previous six. For example, on Monday write 'God is patient' in your diary or on a scrap of paper and tape it to your bathroom mirror or onto the dashboard of your car. On Tuesday write 'God is kind' and so on through the week. And God's promise is this: 'The rain and snow come down from the heavens and stay on the ground to water the earth. They cause the grain to grow, producing seed for the farmer and bread for the hungry. It is the same with my word. I send it out, and it always produces fruit. It will accomplish all I want it to, and it will prosper everywhere I send it' (Is. 55:10–11).

Then do it again for the next two weeks, and for the next two until you fall hopelessly in love with him. Then you will be able to trust again, for even though you are placing your trust in people whom you know may let you down, ultimately your trust is in your Father who, you now know, never will. And that, my friend, is the road to freedom!

## Further Reading

George Bloomer, *Authority Abusers*, Whitaker House, 1995.
Ken Blue, *Healing Spiritual Abuse*, IVP, 1993.
Mike Fehlauer, *Exposing Spiritual Abuse*, Charisma House, 2001.
Marc A. Dupont, *Toxic Churches*, Sovereign World, 2004.
David Johnson & Jeff VanVonderen, *The Subtle Power of Spiritual Abuse*, Bethany House Publishers, 1991.

## Useful websites

www.safeinchurch.co.uk
www.dialogueireland.org
www.savageshepherds.co.uk

# Endnotes

1 Stephen Mansfield, *Derek Prince: A teacher for our time* (Baldock: Derek Prince Ministries), p. 221.

2 Ibid.

3 Derek Prince, *Discipleship, Shepherding, Commitment* (Fort Lauderdale: Derek Prince Publishing, 1976), p. 18.

4 Ibid.

5 Ken Blue, *Healing Spiritual Abuse* (Downers Grove: IVP, 1993).

6 www.3.zondervan.com/features/authors/yancey/bio.htm.

7 http//candler.emory.edu/ABOUT/faculty/long.com.

8 James Strong, *Strong's Exhaustive Concordance of the Bible* (Massachusetts: Hendrickson Publishers, 1993).

9 L. Gregory Jones, *Embodying Forgiveness* (Grand Rapids: Eerdmans, 1995).

10 Marc Dupont, *Toxic Churches* (Tonbridge: Sovereign World, 2004), p. 31.

11 William Cowper 1731–1800.

12 James Hastings, *Dictionary of the Apostlic Church* (Edinburgh: T&T Clark, 1916).

13 *The Encyclopedia Americana* (Americana Corp., 1970).

14 Jake Barnett, *Wealth and Wisdom* (Colorado Springs: Navpress, 1987), p. 192.

121

[15] James Strong, *Strong's Exhaustive Concordance of the Bible.*

[16] Walter A. Elwell, Ed., *Evangelical Dictionary of Biblical Theology* (Grand Rapids: Baker Books, 1996).

[17] Vine, Under, Merrill and White, *Vine's Expository Dictionary of New Testament Words* (Nashville: Thomas Nelson, 1996).

[18] William Cowper 1731–1800.

[19] *Matthew Henry's Commentary: Acts to Revelation*, ed. David Winter (London: Hodder & Stoughton, 1975).

[20] Jack Frost, *Experiencing the Father's Embrace* (Shippensburg: Destiny Image Publishers, 2002).

[21] Ken Blue, *Healing Spiritual Abuse* (Downers Grove: IVP, 1993).

[22] John Powell, *Why Am I Afraid to Love?* (Grand Rapids: Zondervan, 1999).

[23] James Strong, *Strong's Exhaustive Concordance of the Bible.*